THE COLLECTED WORKS OF

WILLIAM BUTLER YEATS

THE HOUR-GLASS. CATHLEEN NI
HOULIHAN. THE GOLDEN HELMET.
THE IRISH DRAMATIC MOVEMENT
♣ BEING THE FOURTH VOLUME OF
THE COLLECTED WORKS IN VERSE &
PROSE OF WILLIAM BUTLER YEATS
IMPRINTED AT THE SHAKESPEARE
HEAD PRESS STRATFORD-ON-AVON
MCMVIII

CONTENTS

THE HOUR-GLASS:

A MORALITY

PERSONS IN THE PLAY

A Wise Man
A Fool
Some Pupils
An Angel
The Wise Man's Wife and two Children

THE HOUR-GLASS:

A MORALITY

A large room with a door at the back and another at the side, or else a curtained place where persons can enter by parting the curtains. A desk and a chair at one side. An hour-glass on a bracket or stand near the door. A creepy stool near it. Some benches. A WISE MAN *sitting at his desk.*

WISE MAN.

[*Turning over the pages of a book.*]

WHERE is that passage I am to explain to my pupils to-day? Here it is, and the book says that it was written by a beggar on the walls of Babylon: 'There are two living countries, the one visible and the one invisible; and when it is winter with us it is summer in that country, and when the November winds are up among us it is lambing-time there.' I wish that my pupils had asked me to explain any other passage. [*The* FOOL *comes in and stands at the door holding out his hat. He has a pair of shears in the other hand.*] It sounds to me like foolishness; and yet that cannot be, for the writer of this book, where I have found so much knowledge, would not have set it by itself on this page, and surrounded it with so many images and so many deep colours and so much fine gilding, if it had been foolishness.

FOOL.

Give me a penny.

WISE MAN [*turns to another page*].

Here he has written: 'The learned in old times forgot the visible country.' That I understand, but I have taught my learners better.

FOOL.

Won't you give me a penny?

WISE MAN.

What do you want? The words of the wise Saracen will not teach you much.

FOOL.

Such a great wise teacher as you are will not refuse a penny to a fool.

WISE MAN.

What do you know about wisdom?

FOOL.

Oh, I know! I know what I have seen.

WISE MAN.

What is it you have seen?

FOOL.

When I went by Kilcluan where the bells used
to be ringing at the break of every day, I could
hear nothing but the people snoring in their
houses. When I went by Tubbervanach, where
the young men used to be climbing the hill to
the blessed well, they were sitting at the cross-
roads playing cards. When I went by Carri-
goras, where the friars used to be fasting and
serving the poor, I saw them drinking wine
and obeying their wives. And when I asked
what misfortune had brought all these changes,
they said it was no misfortune, but it was the
wisdom they had learned from your teaching.

WISE MAN.

Run round to the kitchen, and my wife will
give you something to eat.

FOOL.

That is foolish advice for a wise man to give.

WISE MAN.

Why, Fool?

FOOL.

What is eaten is gone. I want pennies for
my bag. I must buy bacon in the shops, and
nuts in the market, and strong drink for the
time when the sun is weak. And I want snares
to catch the rabbits and the squirrels and the
hares, and a pot to cook them in.

WISE MAN.

Go away. I have other things to think of now than giving you pennies.

FOOL.

Give me a penny and I will bring you luck. Bresal the Fisherman lets me sleep among the nets in his loft in the winter-time because he says I bring him luck; and in the summer-time the wild creatures let me sleep near their nests and their holes. It is lucky even to look at me or to touch me, but it is much more lucky to give me a penny. [*Holds out his hand.*] If I wasn't lucky, I'd starve.

WISE MAN.

What have you got the shears for?

FOOL.

I won't tell you. If I told you, you would drive them away.

WISE MAN.

Whom would I drive away?

FOOL.

I won't tell you.

WISE MAN.

Not if I give you a penny?

FOOL.

No.

WISE MAN.

Not if I give you two pennies?

FOOL.

You will be very lucky if you give me two pennies, but I won't tell you!

WISE MAN.

Three pennies?

FOOL.

Four, and I will tell you!

WISE MAN.

Very well, four. But I will not call you Teig the Fool any longer.

FOOL.

Let me come close to you where nobody will hear me. But first you must promise you will not drive them away. [WISE MAN *nods*.] Every day men go out dressed in black and spread great black nets over the hills, great black nets.

WISE MAN.

Why do they do that?

FOOL.

That they may catch the feet of the angels. But every morning, just before the dawn, I go out and cut the nets with my shears, and the angels fly away.

WISE MAN.

Ah, now I know that you are Teig the Fool. You have told me that I am wise, and I have never seen an angel.

FOOL.

I have seen plenty of angels.

WISE MAN.

Do you bring luck to the angels too?

FOOL.

Oh, no, no! No one could do that. But they are always there if one looks about one; they are like the blades of grass.

WISE MAN.

When do you see them?

FOOL.

When one gets quiet, then something wakes up inside one, something happy and quiet like the stars—not like the seven that move, but like the fixed stars. [*He points upward.*

WISE MAN.

And what happens then?

FOOL.

Then all in a minute one smells summer flowers, and tall people go by, happy and laughing, and their clothes are the colour of burning sods.

WISE MAN.

Is it long since you have seen them, Teig
the Fool?

FOOL.

Not long, glory be to God! I saw one coming
behind me just now. It was not laughing, but
it had clothes the colour of burning sods, and
there was something shining about its head.

WISE MAN.

Well, there are your four pennies. You, a
fool, say 'Glory be to God,' but before I came
the wise men said it.

FOOL.

Four pennies! That means a great deal of
luck. Great teacher, I have brought you plenty
of luck! [*He goes out shaking the bag.*

WISE MAN.

Though they call him Teig the Fool, he
is not more foolish than everybody used to be,
with their dreams and their preachings and
their three worlds; but I have overthrown their
three worlds with the seven sciences. With
Philosophy that was made from the lonely star,
I have taught them to forget Theology; with
Architecture, I have hidden the ramparts of
their cloudy heaven; with Music, the fierce
planets' daughter whose hair is always on fire,

and with Grammar that is the moon's daughter, I have shut their ears to the imaginary harpings and speech of the angels ; and I have made formations of battle with Arithmetic that have put the hosts of heaven to the rout. But, Rhetoric and Dialectic, that have been born out of the light star and out of the amorous star, you have been my spearman and my catapult! Oh! my swift horsemen! Oh! my keen darting arguments, it is because of you that I have overthrown the hosts of foolishness! [*An* ANGEL, *in a dress the colour of embers, and carrying a blossoming apple-bough in her hand and a gilded halo about her head, stands upon the threshold.*] Before I came, men's minds were stuffed with folly about a heaven where birds sang the hours, and about angels that came and stood upon men's thresholds. But I have locked the visions into heaven and turned the key upon them. Well, I must consider this passage about the two countries. My mother used to say something of the kind. She would say that when our bodies sleep our souls awake, and that whatever withers here ripens yonder, and that harvests are snatched from us that they may feed invisible people. But the meaning of the book may be different, for only fools and women have thoughts like that; their thoughts were never written upon the walls of Babylon. I must ring the bell for my pupils. [*He sees the* ANGEL.] What are you? Who are you? I think I saw some that were like you in my dreams when I was a child—that bright thing, that dress that is the colour of embers! But I have done with dreams, I have done with dreams.

ANGEL.

I am the Angel of the Most High God.

WISE MAN.

Why have you come to me?

ANGEL.

I have brought you a message.

WISE MAN.

What message have you got for me?

ANGEL.

You will die within the hour. You will die when the last grains have fallen in this glass.

[*She turns the hour-glass.*

WISE MAN.

My time to die has not come. I have my pupils. I have a young wife and children that I cannot leave. Why must I die?

ANGEL.

You must die because no souls have passed over the threshold of Heaven since you came into this country. The threshold is grassy, and the gates are rusty, and the angels that keep watch there are lonely.

WISE MAN.

Where will death bring me to?

ANGEL.

The doors of Heaven will not open to you, for you have denied the existence of Heaven; and the doors of Purgatory will not open to you, for you have denied the existence of Purgatory.

WISE MAN.

But I have also denied the existence of Hell!

ANGEL.

Hell is the place of those who deny.

WISE MAN [kneels].

I have, indeed, denied everything, and have taught others to deny. I have believed in nothing but what my senses told me. But, oh! beautiful Angel, forgive me, forgive me!

ANGEL.

You should have asked forgiveness long ago.

WISE MAN.

Had I seen your face as I see it now, oh! beautiful angel, I would have believed, I would have asked forgiveness. Maybe you do not know how easy it is to doubt. Storm, death, the grass rotting, many sicknesses, those are the messengers that came to me. Oh! why are you silent? You carry the pardon of the Most High; give it to me! I would kiss your hands if I were not afraid—no, no, the hem of your dress!

ANGEL.

You let go undying hands too long ago to take hold of them now.

WISE MAN.

You cannot understand. You live in a country that we can only dream about. Maybe it is as hard for you to understand why we disbelieve as it is for us to believe. Oh! what have I said! You know everything! Give me time to undo what I have done. Give me a year—a month—a day—an hour! Give me to this hour's end, that I may undo what I have done!

ANGEL.

You cannot undo what you have done. Yet I have this power with my message. If you can find one that believes before the hour's end, you shall come to Heaven after the years of Purgatory. For, from one fiery seed, watched over by those that sent me, the harvest can come again to heap the golden threshing-floor. But now farewell, for I am weary of the weight of time.

WISE MAN.

Blessed be the Father, blessed be the Son, blessed be the Spirit, blessed be the Messenger They have sent!

ANGEL.

[*At the door and pointing at the hour-glass.*]

In a little while the uppermost glass will be empty. [*Goes out.*

WISE MAN.

Everything will be well with me. I will call my pupils; they only say they doubt. [*Pulls the bell.*] They will be here in a moment. They want to please me; they pretend that they disbelieve. Belief is too old to be overcome all in a minute. Besides, I can prove what I once disproved. [*Another pull at the bell.*] They are coming now. I will go to my desk. I will speak quietly, as if nothing had happened.

[*He stands at the desk with a fixed look in his eyes. The voices of* THE PUPILS *are heard singing these words:*

I was going the road one day—
O the brown and the yellow beer—
And I met with a man that was no right man:
O my dear, O my dear!

Enter PUPILS *and the* FOOL.

FOOL.

Leave me alone. Leave me alone. Who is that pulling at my bag? King's son, do not pull at my bag.

A YOUNG MAN.

Did your friends the angels give you that bag? Why don't they fill your bag for you?

FOOL.

Give me pennies! Give me some pennies!

A YOUNG MAN.

What do you want pennies for? that great bag at your waist is heavy.

FOOL.

I want to buy bacon in the shops, and nuts in the market, and strong drink for the time when the sun is weak, and snares to catch rabbits and the squirrels that steal the nuts, and hares, and a great pot to cook them in.

A YOUNG MAN.

Why don't your friends tell you where buried treasures are? Why don't they make you dream about treasures? If one dreams three times there is always treasure.

FOOL [*holding out his hat*].

Give me pennies! Give me pennies!

[*They throw pennies into his hat. He is standing
close to the door, that he may hold out his hat
to each newcomer.*

A YOUNG MAN.

Master, will you have Teig the Fool for a
scholar?

ANOTHER YOUNG MAN.

Teig, will you give us your pennies if we
teach you lessons?   No, he goes to school for
nothing on the mountains.   Tell us what you
learn on the mountains, Teig?

WISE MAN.

Be silent all! [*He has been standing silent, look-
ing away.*] Stand still in your places, for there
is something I would have you tell me.

[*A moment's pause.   They all stand round in
their places.* TEIG *still stands at the door.*

WISE MAN.

Is there any one amongst you who believes
in God? In Heaven? Or in Purgatory? Or
in Hell?

ALL THE YOUNG MEN.

No one, Master! No one!

WISE MAN.

I knew you would all say that; but do not be afraid. I will not be angry. Tell me the truth. Do you not believe?

A YOUNG MAN.

We once did, but you have taught us to know better.

WISE MAN.

Oh! teaching, teaching does not go very deep! The heart remains unchanged under it all. You have the faith that you always had, and you are afraid to tell me.

A YOUNG MAN.

No, no, Master!

WISE MAN.

If you tell me that you have not changed I shall be glad and not angry.

A YOUNG MAN [to his Neighbour].
He wants somebody to dispute with.

HIS NEIGHBOUR.

I knew that from the beginning.

A YOUNG MAN.

That is not the subject for to-day; you were going to talk about the words the beggar wrote upon the walls of Babylon.

WISE MAN.

If there is one amongst you that believes, he will be my best friend. Surely there is one amongst you. [*They are all silent.*] Surely what you learned at your mother's knees has not been so soon forgotten.

A YOUNG MAN.

Master, till you came, no teacher in this land was able to get rid of foolishness and ignorance. But every one has listened to you, every one has learned the truth. You have had your last disputation.

ANOTHER.

What a fool you made of that monk in the market-place! He had not a word to say.

WISE MAN.

[*Comes from his desk and stands among them in the middle of the room.*]

Pupils, dear friends, I have deceived you all this time. It was I myself who was ignorant. There is a God. There is a Heaven. There is fire that passes, and there is fire that lasts for ever.

[TEIG, *through all this, is sitting on a stool by the door, reckoning on his fingers what he will buy with his money.*

A YOUNG MAN [*to* Another.]

He will not be satisfied till we dispute with him. [*To the* WISE MAN.] Prove it, Master. Have you seen them?

WISE MAN [*in a low, solemn voice*].

Just now, before you came in, someone came to the door, and when I looked up I saw an angel standing there.

A YOUNG MAN.

You were in a dream. Anybody can see an angel in his dreams.

WISE MAN.

Oh, my God! It was not a dream! I was awake, waking as I am now. I tell you I was awake as I am now.

A YOUNG MAN.

Some dream when they are awake, but they are the crazy, and who would believe what they say? Forgive me, Master, but that is what you taught me to say. That is what you said to the monk when he spoke of the visions of the saints and the martyrs.

ANOTHER YOUNG MAN.

You see how well we remember your teaching.

WISE MAN.

Out, out from my sight! I want someone
with belief. I must find that grain the Angel
spoke of before I die. I tell you I must find it,
and you answer me with arguments. Out with
you, out of my sight!

[*The* Young Men *laugh.*

A YOUNG MAN.

How well he plays at faith! He is like the
monk when he had nothing more to say.

WISE MAN.

Out, out! This is no time for laughter! Out
with you, though you are a king's son!

[*They begin to hurry out.*

A YOUNG MAN.

Come, come; he wants us to find someone
who will dispute with him. [*All go out.*

WISE MAN.

[*Alone; he goes to the door at the side.*]
I will call my wife. She will believe; women
always believe. [*He opens the door and calls.*]
Bridget! Bridget! [BRIDGET *comes in wearing
her apron, her sleeves turned up from her floury
arms.*] Bridget, tell me the truth; do not say
what you think will please me. Do you some-
times say your prayers?

BRIDGET.

Prayers! No, you taught me to leave them off long ago. At first I was sorry, but I am glad now for I am sleepy in the evenings.

WISE MAN.

But do you not believe in God?

BRIDGET.

Oh, a good wife only believes what her husband tells her!

WISE MAN.

But sometimes when you are alone, when I am in the school and the children asleep, do you not think about the saints, about the things you used to believe in? What do you think of when you are alone?

BRIDGET [considering].

I think about nothing. Sometimes I wonder if the linen is bleaching white, or I go out to see if the crows are picking up the chickens' food.

WISE MAN.

Oh, what can I do! Is there nobody who believes he can never die? I must go and find somebody! [He goes towards the door, but stops with his eyes fixed on the hour-glass.] I cannot go out; I cannot leave that. Go, and call my pupils again. I will make them understand. I will say to them that only amid spiritual terror, or only when all that laid hold on life is shaken can we see truth. There is something in Plato, but—no, do not call them. They would answer as I have bid.

BRIDGET.

You want somebody to get up an argument with.

WISE MAN.

Oh, look out of the door and tell me if there is anybody there in the street. I cannot leave this glass; somebody might shake it! Then the sand would fall more quickly.

BRIDGET.

I don't understand what you are saying. [*Looks out.*] There is a great crowd of people talking to your pupils.

WISE MAN.

Oh, run out, Bridget, and see if they have found somebody that all the time I was teaching understood nothing or did not listen!

BRIDGET.

[*Wiping her arms in her apron and pulling down her sleeves.*]

It's a hard thing to be married to a man of learning that must be always having arguments. [*Goes out and shouts through the kitchen aoor.*] Don't be meddling with the bread, children, while I'm out.

WISE MAN [*kneels down*].

'*Confiteor Deo Omnipotenti beatæ Mariæ* . .
I have forgotten it all. It is thirty years since I
have said a prayer. I must pray in the common
tongue, like a clown begging in the market,
like Teig the Fool! [*He prays*]. Help me,
Father, Son, and Spirit!

[BRIDGET *enters, followed by the* FOOL, *who is holding out his hat to her.*

FOOL.

Give me something; give me a penny to buy
bacon in the shops, and nuts in the market,
and strong drink for the time when the sun
grows weak.

BRIDGET.

I have no pennies. [*To the* WISE MAN.]
Your pupils cannot find anybody to argue with
you. There is nobody in the whole country who
has enough belief to fill a pipe with since you
put down the monk. Can't you be quiet now
and not always wanting to have arguments?
It must be terrible to have a mind like that.

WISE MAN.

I am lost! I am lost!

BRIDGET.

Leave me alone now; I have to make the
bread for you and the children.

WISE MAN.

Out of this, woman, out of this, I say!
[BRIDGET *goes through the kitchen door.*] Will
nobody find a way to help me! But she spoke
of my children. I had forgotten them. They
will believe. It is only those who have reason
that doubt; the young are full of faith. Bridget,
Bridget, send my children to me.

BRIDGET [*inside*].

Your father wants you; run to him now.

[*The two* CHILDREN *come in. They stand together
a little way from the threshold of the kitchen
door, looking timidly at their father.*

WISE MAN.

Children, what do you believe?   Is there a
Heaven? Is there a Hell? Is there a Purgatory?

FIRST CHILD.

We haven't forgotten, father.

THE OTHER CHILD.

O no, father. [*They both speak together as if
in school.*] There is nothing we cannot see;
there is nothing we cannot touch.

FIRST CHILD.

Foolish people used to think that there was,
but you are very learned and you have taught
us better.

WISE MAN.

You are just as bad as the others, just as bad as the others! Do not run away, come back to me! [*The* CHILDREN *begin to cry and run away.*] Why are you afraid? I will teach you better— no, I will never teach you again. Go to your mother! no, she will not be able to teach them . . . Help them, O God! . . . The grains are going very quickly. There is very little sand in the uppermost glass. Somebody will come for me in a moment; perhaps he is at the door now! All creatures that have reason doubt. O that the grass and the plants could speak! Somebody has said that they would wither if they doubted. O speak to me, O grass blades! O fingers of God's certainty, speak to me! You are millions and you will not speak. I dare not know the moment the messenger will come for me. I will cover the glass. [*He covers it and brings it to the desk. Sees the* FOOL, *who is sitting by the door playing with some flowers which he has stuck in his hat. He has begun to blow a dandelion-head.*] What are you doing?

FOOL.

Wait a moment. [*He blows.*] Four, five, six.

WISE MAN.

What are you doing that for?

FOOL.

I am blowing at the dandelion to find out what time it is.

WISE MAN.

You have heard everything! That is why you want to find out what hour it is! You are waiting to see them coming through the door to carry me away. [FOOL *goes on blowing*.] Out through the door with you! I will have no one here when they come. [*He seizes the* FOOL *by the shoulders, and begins to force him out through the door, then suddenly changes his mind.*] No, I have something to ask you. [*He drags him back into the room.*] Is there a Heaven? Is there a Hell? Is there a Purgatory?

FOOL.

So you ask me now. When you were asking your pupils, I said to myself, if he would ask Teig the Fool, Teig could tell him all about it, for Teig has learned all about it when he has been cutting the nets.

WISE MAN.

Tell me; tell me!

FOOL.

I said, Teig knows everything. Not even the cats or the hares that milk the cows have Teig's wisdom. But Teig will not speak; he says nothing.

WISE MAN.

Tell me, tell me! For under the cover the grains are falling, and when they are all fallen I shall die; and my soul will be lost if I have not found somebody that believes! Speak, speak!

FOOL [*looking wise*].

No, no, I won't tell you what is in my mind, and I won't tell you what is in my bag. You might steal away my thoughts. I met a bodach on the road yesterday, and he said, 'Teig, tell me how many pennies are in your bag; I will wager three pennies that there are not twenty pennies in your bag; let me put in my hand and count them.' But I pulled the strings tighter, like this; and when I go to sleep every night I hide the bag where no one knows.

WISE MAN.

[*Goes towards the hour-glass as if to uncover it.*]

No, no, I have not the courage. [*He kneels.*] Have pity upon me, Fool, and tell me!

FOOL.

Ah! Now, that is different. I am not afraid of you now. But I must come nearer to you; somebody in there might hear what the Angel said.

WISE MAN.

Oh, what did the Angel tell you?

FOOL.

Once I was alone on the hills, and an angel came by and he said, 'Teig the Fool, do not forget the Three Fires; the Fire that punishes, the Fire that purifies, and the Fire wherein the soul rejoices for ever!'

WISE MAN.

He believes! I am saved! The sand has run out. . . . [FOOL *helps him to his chair.*] I am going from the country of the seven wandering stars, and I am going to the country of the fixed stars! I understand it all now. One sinks in on God; we do not see the truth; God sees the truth in us. Ring the bell. They are coming. Tell them, Fool, that when the life and the mind are broken the truth comes through them like peas through a broken peascod. Pray, Fool, that they may be given a sign and carry their souls alive out of the dying world. Your prayers are better than mine.

[FOOL *bows his head.* WISE MAN's *head sinks on his arm on the books.* PUPILS *are heard singing as before, but now they come right on to the stage before they cease their song.*

A YOUNG MAN.

Look at the Fool turned bell-ringer!

ANOTHER.

What have you called us in for, Teig? What are you going to tell us?

ANOTHER.

No wonder he has had dreams! See, he is fast asleep now. [*Goes over and touches him.*] Oh, he is dead!

FOOL.

Do not stir! He asked for a sign that you might be saved. [*All are silent for a moment.*] . . Look what has come from his mouth. . . a little winged thing . . . a little shining thing. . . It is gone to the door. [*The* ANGEL *appears in the doorway, stretches out her hands and closes them again.*] The Angel has taken it in her hands. . . . She will open her hands in the Garden of Paradise. [*They all kneel.*

PERSONS IN THE PLAY

PETER GILLANE

MICHAEL GILLANE, *his Son, going to be married*

PATRICK GILLANE, *a lad of twelve, Michael's Brother*

BRIDGET GILLANE, *Peter's Wife*

DELIA CAHEL, *engaged to Michael*

THE POOR OLD WOMAN

Neighbours

CATHLEEN NI HOULIHAN

Interior of a cottage close to Killala, in 1798.
BRIDGET *is standing at a table undoing a parcel.*
PETER *is sitting at one side of the fire,* PATRICK
at the other.

PETER.

WHAT is that sound I hear?

PATRICK.

I don't hear anything. [*He listens.*] I hear
it now. It's like cheering. [*He goes to the window
and looks out.*] I wonder what they are cheering
about. I don't see anybody.

PETER.

It might be a hurling.

PATRICK.

There's no hurling to-day. It must be down
in the town the cheering is.

BRIDGET.

I suppose the boys must be having some
sport of their own. Come over here, Peter, and
look at Michael's wedding-clothes.

PETER [*shifts his chair to table*].
Those are grand clothes, indeed.

BRIDGET.
You hadn't clothes like that when you married me, and no coat to put on of a Sunday more than any other day.

PETER.
That is true, indeed. We never thought a son of our own would be wearing a suit of that sort for his wedding, or have so good a place to bring a wife to.

PATRICK [*who is still at the window*].
There's an old woman coming down the road. I don't know is it here she is coming?

BRIDGET.
It will be a neighbour coming to hear about Michael's wedding. Can you see who it is?

PATRICK.
I think it is a stranger, but she's not coming to the house. She's turned into the gap that goes down where Murteen and his sons are shearing sheep. [*He turns towards* BRIDGET.] Do you remember what Winny of the Cross Roads was saying the other night about the strange woman that goes through the country whatever time there's war or trouble coming?

BRIDGET.

Don't be bothering us about Winny's talk, but go and open the door for your brother. I hear him coming up the path.

PETER.

I hope he has brought Delia's fortune with him safe, for fear her ·people might go back on the bargain and I after making it. Trouble enough I had making it.

[PATRICK *opens the door and* MICHAEL *comes in.*

BRIDGET.

What kept you, Michael? We were looking out for you this long time.

MICHAEL.

I went round by the priest's house to bid him be ready to marry us to-morrow.

BRIDGET.

Did he say anything?

MICHAEL.

He said it was a very nice match, and that he was never better pleased to marry any two in his parish than myself and Delia Cahel.

PETER.

Have you got the fortune, Michael?

MICHAEL.

Here it is.

[MICHAEL *puts bag on table and goes over and leans against chimney-jamb.* BRIDGET, *who has been all this time examining the clothes, pulling the seams and trying the lining of the pockets, etc., puts the clothes on the dresser.*

PETER.

[*Getting up and taking the bag in his hand and turning out the money.*]

Yes, I made the bargain well for you, Michael. Old John Cahel would sooner have kept a share of this a while longer. 'Let me keep the half of it until the first boy is born,' says he. 'You will not,' says I. 'Whether there is or is not a boy, the whole hundred pounds must be in Michael's hands before he brings your daughter to the house.' The wife spoke to him then, and he gave in at the end.

BRIDGET.

You seem well pleased to be handling the money, Peter.

PETER.

Indeed, I wish I had had the luck to get a hundred pounds, or twenty pounds itself, with the wife I married.

BRIDGET.

Well, if I didn't bring much I didn't get much. What had you the day I married you but a flock of hens and you feeding them, and a few lambs and you driving them to the market at Ballina. [*She is vexed and bangs a jug on the dresser.*] If I brought no fortune I worked it out in my bones, laying down the baby, Michael that is standing there now, on a stook of straw, while I dug the potatoes, and never asking big dresses or anything but to be working.

PETER.

That is true, indeed. [*He pats her arm.*

BRIDGET.

Leave me alone now till I ready the house for the woman that is to come into it.

PETER.

You are the best woman in Ireland, but money is good, too. [*He begins handling the money again and sits down.*] I never thought to see so much money within my four walls. We can do great things now we have it. We can take the ten acres of land we have a chance of since Jamsie Dempsey died, and stock it. We will go to the fair of Ballina to buy the stock. Did Delia ask any of the money for her own use, Michael?

MICHAEL.

She did not, indeed. She did not seem to take much notice of it, or to look at it at all.

BRIDGET.

That's no wonder.   Why would she look
at it when she had yourself to look at, a fine,
strong young man? it is proud she must be to
get you; a good steady boy that will make use
of the money, and not be running through it
or spending it on drink like another.

PETER.

It's likely Michael himself was not thinking
much of the fortune either, but of what sort
the girl was to look at.

MICHAEL [*coming over towards the table*].

Well, you would like a nice comely girl to
be beside you, and to go walking with you.
The fortune only lasts for a while, but the
woman will be there always.

PATRICK [*turning round from the window*].

They are cheering again down in the town.
Maybe they are landing horses from Enniscrone.
They do be cheering when the horses take the
water well.

MICHAEL.

There are no horses in it.   Where would
they be going and no fair at hand?   Go down
to the town, Patrick, and see what is going on.

PATRICK.

[*Opens the door to go out, but stops for a moment on the threshold.*]

Will Delia remember, do you think, to bring the greyhound pup she promised me when she would be coming to the house?

MICHAEL.

She will surely.

[PATRICK *goes out, leaving the door open.*

PETER.

It will be Patrick's turn next to be looking for a fortune, but he won't find it so easy to get it and he with no place of his own.

BRIDGET.

I do be thinking sometimes, now things are going so well with us, and the Cahels such a good back to us in the district, and Delia's own uncle a priest, we might be put in the way of making Patrick a priest some day, and he so good at his books.

PETER.

Time enough, time enough, you have always your head full of plans, Bridget.

BRIDGET.

We will be well able to give him learning, and not to send him tramping the country like a poor scholar that lives on charity.

MICHAEL.

They're not done cheering yet.

[*He goes over to the door and stands there for a moment, putting up his hand to shade his eyes.*

BRIDGET.

Do you see anything?

MICHAEL.

I see an old woman coming up the path.

BRIDGET.

Who is it, I wonder? It must be the strange woman Patrick saw a while ago.

MICHAEL.

I don't think it's one of the neighbours anyway, but she has her cloak over her face.

BRIDGET.

It might be some poor woman heard we were making ready for the wedding and came to look for her share.

PETER.

I may as well put the money out of sight. There is no use leaving it out for every stranger to look at.

[*He goes over to a large box in the corner, opens it and puts the bag in and fumbles at the lock.*

MICHAEL.

There she is, father! [*An* Old Woman *passes the window slowly, she looks at* MICHAEL *as she passes.*] I'd sooner a stranger not to come to the house the night before my wedding.

BRIDGET.

Open the door, Michael; don't keep the poor woman waiting.

[*The* OLD WOMAN *comes in.* MICHAEL *stands aside to make way for her.*

OLD WOMAN.

God save all here!

PETER.

God save you kindly!

OLD WOMAN.

You have good shelter here.

PETER.

You are welcome to whatever shelter we have.

BRIDGET.

Sit down there by the fire and welcome.

OLD WOMAN [*warming her hands*].

There is a hard wind outside.

[MICHAEL *watches her curiously from the door.* PETER *comes over to the table.*

PETER.

Have you travelled far to-day?

OLD WOMAN.

I have travelled far, very far; there are few have travelled so far as myself, and there's many a one that doesn't make me welcome. There was one that had strong sons I thought were friends of mine, but they were shearing their sheep, and they wouldn't listen to me.

PETER.

It's a pity indeed for any person to have no place of their own.

OLD WOMAN.

That's true for you indeed, and it's long I'm on the roads since I first went wandering.

BRIDGET.

It is a wonder you are not worn out with so much wandering.

OLD WOMAN.

Sometimes my feet are tired and my hands are quiet, but there is no quiet in my heart. When the people see me quiet, they think old age has come on me and that all the stir has gone out of me. But when the trouble is on me I must be talking to my friends.

BRIDGET.

What was it put you wandering?

OLD WOMAN.

Too many strangers in the house.

BRIDGET.

Indeed you look as if you'd had your share of trouble.

OLD WOMAN.

I have had trouble indeed.

BRIDGET.

What was it put the trouble on you?

OLD WOMAN.

My land that was taken from me.

PETER.

Was it much land they took from you?

OLD WOMAN.

My four beautiful green fields.

PETER [*aside to* BRIDGET].

Do you think could she be the widow Casey that was put out of her holding at Kilglass a while ago?

BRIDGET.

She is not. I saw the widow Casey one time at the market in Ballina, a stout fresh woman.

PETER [*to* OLD WOMAN].

Did you hear a noise of cheering, and you coming up the hill?

OLD WOMAN.

I thought I heard the noise I used to hear when my friends came to visit me.

[*She begins singing half to herself.*

I will go cry with the woman,
For yellow-haired Donough is dead,
With a hempen rope for a neckcloth,
And a white cloth on his head,——

MICHAEL [*coming from the door*].

What is that you are singing, ma'am?

OLD WOMAN.

Singing I am about a man I knew one time, yellow-haired Donough that was hanged in Galway.   [*She goes on singing, much louder.*

I am come to cry with you, woman,
My hair is unwound and unbound;
I remember him ploughing his field,
Turning up the red side of the ground,

And building his barn on the hill
With the good mortared stone;
O! we'd have pulled down the gallows
Had it happened in Enniscrone!

MICHAEL.

What was it brought him to his death?

OLD WOMAN.

He died for love of me: many a man has died for love of me.

PETER [*aside to* BRIDGET].
Her trouble has put her wits astray.

MICHAEL.
Is it long since that song was made?   Is it long since he got his death?

OLD WOMAN.
Not long, not long.   But there were others that died for love of me a long time ago.

MICHAEL.
Were they neighbours of your own, ma'am?

OLD WOMAN.
Come here beside me and I'll tell you about them. [MICHAEL *sits down beside her at the hearth.*] There was a red man of the O'Donnells from the north, and a man of the O'Sullivans from the south, and there was one Brian that lost his life at Clontarf by the sea, and there were a great many in the west, some that died hundreds of years ago, and there are some that will die to-morrow.

MICHAEL.
Is it in the west that men will die to-morrow?

OLD WOMAN.
Come nearer, nearer to me.

BRIDGET.
Is she right, do you think?   Or is she a woman from beyond the world?

PETER.

She doesn't know well what she's talking about, with the want and the trouble she has gone through.

BRIDGET.

The poor thing, we should treat her well.

PETER.

Give her a drink of milk and a bit of the oaten cake.

BRIDGET.

Maybe we should give her something along with that, to bring her on her way. A few pence or a shilling itself, and we with so much money in the house.

PETER.

Indeed I'd not begrudge it to her if we had it to spare, but if we go running through what we have, we'll soon have to break the hundred pounds, and that would be a pity.

BRIDGET.

Shame on you, Peter. Give her the shilling and your blessing with it, or our own luck will go from us.

[PETER *goes to the box and takes out a shilling.*

BRIDGET [*to the* OLD WOMAN].

Will you have a drink of milk, ma'am?

OLD WOMAN.

It is not food or drink that I want.

PETER [*offering the shilling*].
Here is something for you.

OLD WOMAN.
This is not what I want. It is not silver I want.

PETER.
What is it you would be asking for?

OLD WOMAN.
If anyone would give me help he must give
me himself, he must give me all.

[PETER *goes over to the table staring at the
shilling in his hand in a bewildered way, and
stands whispering to* BRIDGET.

MICHAEL.
Have you no one to care you in your age,
ma'am?

OLD WOMAN.
I have not. With all the lovers that brought
me their love, I never set out the bed for any.

MICHAEL.
Are you lonely going the roads, ma'am?

OLD WOMAN.
I have my thoughts and I have my hopes.

MICHAEL.
What hopes have you to hold to?

OLD WOMAN.
The hope of getting my beautiful fields back
again; the hope of putting the strangers out of
my house.

MICHAEL.

What way will you do that, ma'am?

OLD WOMAN.

I have good friends that will help me. They are gathering to help me now. I am not afraid. If they are put down to-day they will get the upper hand to-morrow. [*She gets up.*] I must be going to meet my friends. They are coming to help me and I must be there to welcome them. I must call the neighbours together to welcome them.

MICHAEL.

I will go with you.

BRIDGET.

It is not her friends you have to go and welcome, Michael; it is the girl coming into the house you have to welcome. You have plenty to do, it is food and drink you have to bring to the house. The woman that is coming home is not coming with empty hands; you would not have an empty house before her. [*To the* OLD WOMAN.] Maybe you don't know, ma'am, that my son is going to be married to-morrow.

OLD WOMAN.

It is not a man going to his marriage that I look to for help.

PETER [*to* BRIDGET].

Who is she, do you think, at all?

BRIDGET.

You did not tell us your name yet, ma'am.

OLD WOMAN.

Some call me the Poor Old Woman, and there are some that call me Cathleen, the daughter of Houlihan.

PETER.

I think I knew someone of that name once. Who was it, I wonder? It must have been someone I knew when I was a boy. No, no; I remember, I heard it in a song.

OLD WOMAN.

[*Who is standing in the doorway.*]

They are wondering that there were songs made for me; there have been many songs made for me. I heard one on the wind this morning.

[*Sings.*] Do not make a great keening
When the graves have been dug to-morrow.
Do not call the white-scarfed riders
To the burying that shall be to-morrow.
Do not spread food to call strangers
To the wakes that shall be to-morrow;
Do not give money for prayers
For the dead that shall die to-morrow. . .

they will have no need of prayers, they will have no need of prayers.

E

MICHAEL.

I do not know what that song means, but tell me something I can do for you.

PETER.

Come over to me, Michael.

MICHAEL.

Hush, father, listen to her.

OLD WOMAN.

It is a hard service they take that help me. Many that are red-cheeked now will be pale-cheeked; many that have been free to walk the hills and the bogs and the rushes, will be sent to walk hard streets in far countries; many a good plan will be broken; many that have gathered money will not stay to spend it; many a child will be born and there will be no father at its christening to give it a name.   They that had red cheeks will have pale cheeks for my sake; and for all that, they will think they are well paid.

[*She goes out; her voice is heard outside singing.*

They shall be remembered for ever,
They shall be alive for ever,
They shall be speaking for ever,
The people shall hear them for ever.

BRIDGET [*to* PETER].

Look at him, Peter; he has the look of a man that has got the touch. [*Raising her voice.*] Look here, Michael, at the wedding clothes.

Such grand clothes as these are! You have a right to fit them on now, it would be a pity to-morrow if they did not fit. The boys would be laughing at you. Take them, Michael, and go into the room and fit them on.

[*She puts them on his arm.*

MICHAEL.

What wedding are you talking of? What clothes will I be wearing to-morrow?

BRIDGET.

These are the clothes you are going to wear when you marry Delia Cahel to-morrow.

MICHAEL.

I had forgotten that.

[*He looks at the clothes and turns towards the inner room, but stops at the sound of cheering outside.*

PETER.

There is the shouting come to our own door. What is it has happened?

[Neighbours *come crowding in,* PATRICK *and* DELIA *with them.*

PATRICK.

There are ships in the Bay; the French are landing at Killala!

[PETER *takes his pipe from his mouth and his hat off, and stands up. The clothes slip from* MICHAEL'S *arm.*

DELIA.

Michael! [*He takes no notice.*] Michael! [*He turns towards her.*] Why do you look at me like a stranger?

[*She drops his arm.* BRIDGET *goes over towards her.*

PATRICK.

The boys are all hurrying down the hill-sides to join the French.

DELIA.

Michael won't be going to join the French.

BRIDGET [*to* PETER].

Tell him not to go, Peter.

PETER.

It's no use.   He doesn't hear a word we're saying.

BRIDGET.

Try and coax him over to the fire.

DELIA.

Michael, Michael!   You won't leave me! You won't join the French, and we going to be married!

[*She puts her arms about him, he turns towards her as if about to yield.*

OLD WOMAN'S *voice outside.*

They shall be speaking for ever,
The people shall hear them for ever.

[MICHAEL *breaks away from* DELIA, *stands for a second at the door, then rushes out, following the* OLD WOMAN'S *voice.* BRIDGET *takes* DELIA, *who is crying silently, into her arms.*

PETER.

[*To* PATRICK, *laying a hand on his arm.*]

Did you see an old woman going down the path?

PATRICK.

I did not, but I saw a young girl, and she had the walk of a queen.

PERSONS IN THE PLAY

CUCHULAIN
LEAGERIE
CONAL
EMER, *Cuchulain's wife*
LEAGERIE'S WIFE
CONAL'S WIFE
LAEG, *Cuchulain's chariot-driver*
RED MAN
HORSEBOYS AND SCULLIONS
THREE BLACK MEN

THE GOLDEN HELMET

A house made of logs. There are two windows at the back and a door which cuts off one of the corners of the room. Through the door one can see rocks, which make the ground outside the door higher than it is within, and the sea. Through the windows one can see nothing but the sea. There are three great chairs at the opposite side to the door, with a table before them. There are cups and a flagon of ale on the table.

At the Abbey Theatre the house is orange red, and the chairs, tables and flagons black, with a slight purple tinge which is not clearly distinguishable from the black. The rocks are black, with a few green touches. The sea is green and luminous, and all the characters, except the RED MAN *and the* Black Men *are dressed in various tints of green, one or two with touches of purple which looks nearly black. The* Black Men *are in dark purple and the* RED MAN *is altogether dressed in red. He is very tall and his height is increased by horns on the Golden Helmet. The Helmet has in reality more dark green than gold about it. The* Black Men *have cats' heads painted on their black cloth caps. The effect is intentionally violent and startling.*

CONAL.

Not a sail, not a wave, and if the sea were not purring a little like a cat, not a sound. There is no danger yet. I can see a long way for the moonlight is on the sea.   [*A horn sounds.*

LEAGERIE.

Ah, there is something.

CONAL.

It must be from the land, and it is from the sea that danger comes. We need not be afraid of anything that comes from the land. [*Looking out of door.*] I cannot see anybody, the rocks and the trees hide a great part of the pathway upon that side.

LEAGERIE [*sitting at table*].

It sounded like Cuchulain's horn, but that's not possible.

CONAL.

Yes, that's impossible. He will never come home from Scotland. He has all he wants there. Luck in all he does. Victory and wealth and happiness flowing in on him, while here at home all goes to rack, and a man's good name drifts away between night and morning.

LEAGERIE.

I wish he would come home for all that, and put quiet and respect for those that are more than she is into that young wife of his. Only this very night your wife and my wife had to forbid her to go into the dining-hall before them. She is young, and she is Cuchulain's wife, and so she must spread her tail like a peacock.

CONAL [*at door*].

I can see the horn-blower now, a young man wrapped in a cloak.

LEAGERIE.

Do not let him come in. Tell him to go elsewhere for shelter. This is no place to seek shelter in.

CONAL.

That is right. I will tell him to go away, for nobody must know the disgrace that is to fall upon Ireland this night.

LEAGERIE.

Nobody of living men but us two must ever know that.

CONAL [*outside door*].

Go away, go away!

[*A* YOUNG MAN *covered by a long cloak is standing upon the rocks outside door.*

YOUNG MAN.

I am a traveller, and I am looking for sleep and food.

CONAL.

A law has been made that nobody is to come into this house to-night.

YOUNG MAN.

Who made that law?

CONAL.

We two made it, and who has so good a right? for we have to guard this house and to keep it from robbery, and from burning and from enchantment.

YOUNG MAN.

Then I will unmake the law. Out of my way!

[*He struggles with* CONAL *and shoves past into the house.*

CONAL.

I thought no living man but Leagerie could have stood against me; and Leagerie himself could not have shoved past me. What is more, no living man could if I were not taken by surprise. How could I expect to find so great a strength?

LEAGERIE.

Go out of this: there is another house a little
further along the shore; our wives are there
with their servants, and they will give you food
and drink.

YOUNG MAN.

It is in this house I will have food and drink.

LEAGERIE [*drawing his sword*].

Go out of this, or I will make you.

[*The* YOUNG MAN *seizes* LEAGERIE'S *arm, and
thrusting it up, passes him, and puts his shield
over the chair where there is an empty place.*

YOUNG MAN [*at table*].

It is here I will spend the night, but I won't
tell you why till I have drunk. I am thirsty.
What, the flagon full and the cups empty and
Leagerie and Conal there! Why, what's in the
wind that Leagerie and Conal cannot drink?

LEAGERIE.

It is Cuchulain.

CONAL.

Better go away to Scotland again, or if you
stay here ask no one what has happened or what
is going to happen.

CUCHULAIN.

What more is there that can happen so strange
as that I should come home after years and that
you should bid me begone?

CONAL.

I tell you that this is no fit house to welcome you, for it is a disgraced house.

CUCHULAIN.

What is it you are hinting at? You were sitting there with ale beside you and the door open, and quarrelsome thoughts. You are waiting for something or someone. It is for some messenger who is to bring you to some spoil, or to some adventure that you will keep for yourselves.

LEAGERIE.

Better tell him, for he has such luck that it may be his luck will amend ours.

CONAL.

Yes, I had better tell him, for even now at this very door we saw what luck he had. He had the slope of the ground to help him. Is the sea quiet?

LEAGERIE [*looks out of window*].

There is nothing stirring.

CONAL.

Cuchulain, a little after you went out of this country we were sitting here drinking. We were merry. It was late, close on to midnight, when a strange-looking man with red hair and a great sword in his hand came in through that

door. He asked for ale and we gave it to him,
for we were tired of drinking with one another.
He became merry, and for every joke we made
he made a better, and presently we all three
got up and danced, and then we sang, and then
he said he would show us a new game. He
said he would stoop down and that one of us
was to cut off his head, and afterwards one of
us, or whoever had a mind for the game, was
to stoop down and have his head whipped off.
'You take off my head,' said he, 'and then I
take off his head, and that will be a bargain
and a debt between us. A head for a head, that
is the game,' said he. We laughed at him and
told him he was drunk, for how could he whip
off a head when his own had been whipped off?
Then he began abusing us and calling us names,
so I ran at him and cut his head off, and the
head went on laughing where it lay, and presently
he caught it up in his hands and ran out and
plunged into the sea.

CUCHULAIN [*laughs*].

I have imagined as good, when I had as much
ale, and believed it too.

LEAGERIE [*at table*].

I tell you, Cuchulain, you never did. You
never imagined a story like this.

CONAL.

Why must you be always putting yourself up against Leagerie and myself? and what is more, it was no imagination at all. We said to ourselves that all came out of the flagon, and we laughed, and we said we will tell nobody about it. We made an oath to tell nobody. But twelve months after when we were sitting by this table, the flagon between us—

LEAGERIE.

But full up to the brim—

CONAL.

The thought of that story had put us from our drinking—

LEAGERIE.

We were telling it over to one another—

CONAL.

Suddenly that man came in with his head on his shoulders again, and the big sword in his hand. He asked for payment of his debt, and because neither I nor Leagerie would let him cut off our heads he began abusing us and making little of us, and saying that we were a disgrace, and that all Ireland was disgraced because of us. We had not a word to say.

LEAGERIE.

If you had been here you would have been as silent as we were.

CONAL.

At last he said he would come again in twelve months and give us one more chance to keep our word and pay our debt. After that he went down into the sea again. Will he tell the whole world of the disgrace that has come upon us, do you think?

CUCHULAIN.

Whether he does or does not, we will stand there in the door with our swords out and drive him down to the sea again.

CONAL.

What is the use of fighting with a man whose head laughs when it has been cut off?

LEAGERIE.

We might run away, but he would follow us everywhere.

CONAL.

He is coming; the sea is beginning to splash and rumble as it did before he came the last time.

CUCHULAIN.

Let us shut the door and put our backs against it.

F

LEAGERIE.

It is too late. Look, there he is at the door.
He is standing on the threshold.

[*A* MAN *dressed in red, with a great sword and
red ragged hair, and having a Golden Helmet
on his head, is standing on the threshold.*

CUCHULAIN.

Go back into the sea, old red head! If you
will take off heads, take off the head of the sea
turtle of Muirthemne, or of the pig of Con-
naught that has a moon in his belly, or of that
old juggler Manannan, son of the sea, or of the
red man of the Boyne, or of the King of the
Cats, for they are of your own sort, and it may
be they understand your ways. Go, I say, for
when a man's head is off it does not grow again.
What are you standing there for? Go down, I
say. If I cannot harm you with the sword I
will put you down into the sea with my hands.
Do you laugh at me, old red head? Go down
before I lay my hands upon you.

RED MAN.

So you also believe I was in earnest when I
asked for a man's head? It was but a drinker's
joke, an old juggling feat, to pass the time. I
am the best of all drinkers and tipsy companions,
the kindest there is among the Shape-changers

of the world. Look, I have brought this Golden
Helmet as a gift. It is for you or for Leagerie
or for Conal, for the best man, and the bravest
fighting-man amongst you, and you yourselves
shall choose the man. Leagerie is brave, and
Conal is brave. They risk their lives in battle,
but they were not brave enough for my jokes
and my juggling. [*He lays the Golden Helmet on
the ground.*] Have I been too grim a joker?
Well, I am forgiven now, for there is the
Helmet, and let the strongest take it.

[*He goes out.*

CONAL [*taking Helmet*].

It is my right. I am a year older than
Leagerie, and I have fought in more battles.

LEAGERIE [*strutting about stage, sings*].

Leagerie of the Battles
Has put to the sword
The cat-headed men
And carried away
Their hidden gold.

[*He snatches Helmet at the last word.*

CONAL.

Give it back to me, I say. What was the
treasure but withered leaves when you got to
your own door?

CUCHULAIN.

[*Taking the Helmet from* LEAGERIE.]
Give it to me, I say.

CONAL.

You are too young, Cuchulain. What deeds
have you to be set beside our deeds?

CUCHULAIN.

I have not taken it for myself. It will belong
to us all equally. [*He goes to table and begins
filling Helmet with ale.*] We will pass it round
and drink out of it turn about and no one will
be able to claim that it belongs to him more
than another. I drink to your wife, Conal,
and to your wife, Leagerie, and I drink to
Emer my own wife. [*Shouting and blowing of
horns in the distance.*] What is that noise?

CONAL.

It is the horseboys and the huntboys and
the scullions quarrelling. I know the sound,
for I have heard it often of late. It is a good
thing that you are home, Cuchulain, for it is
your own horseboy and chariot-driver, Laeg,
that is the worst of all, and now you will keep
him quiet. They take down the great hunting-
horns when they cannot drown one another's
voices by shouting. There—there—do you
hear them now? [*Shouting so as to be heard
above the noise.*] I drink to your good health,

Cuchulain, and to your young wife, though it were well if she did not quarrel with my wife.

Many men, among whom is LAEG, *chariot-driver of* CUCHULAIN, *come in with great horns of many fantastic shapes.*

LAEG.

I am Cuchulain's chariot-driver, and I say that my master is the best.

ANOTHER.

He is not, but Leagerie is.

ANOTHER.

No, but Conal is.

LAEG.

Make them listen to me, Cuchulain.

ANOTHER.

No, but listen to me.

LAEG.

When I said Cuchulain should have the Helmet, they blew the horns.

ANOTHER.

Conal has it.   The best man has it.

CUCHULAIN.

Silence, all of you.   What is all this uproar, Laeg, and who began it?

[*The* Scullions *and the* Horseboys *point at* LAEG *and cry,* 'He began it.' *They keep up an all but continual murmur through what follows.*

LAEG.

A man with a red beard came where we were sitting, and as he passed me he cried out that they were taking a golden helmet or some such thing from you and denying you the championship of Ireland.   I stood up on that and I cried out that you were the best of the men of Ireland.   But the others cried for Leagerie or Conal, and because I have a big voice they got down the horns to drown my voice, and as neither I nor they would keep silent we have come here to settle it.   I demand that the Helmet be taken from Conal and be given to you.

   [*The* Horseboys *and the* Scullions *shout*, 'No,
     no; give it to Leagerie,' 'The best man
     has it,' *etc.*

CUCHULAIN.

It has not been given to Conal or to anyone. I have made it into a drinking-cup that it may belong to all.   I drank and then Conal drank. Give it to Leagerie, Conal, that he may drink. That will make them see that it belongs to all of us.

A SCULLION OR HORSEBOY.

Cuchulain is right.

ANOTHER.

Cuchulain is right, and I am tired blowing on the big horn.

LAEG.

Cuchulain, you drank first.

ANOTHER.

He gives it to Leagerie now, but he has taken the honour of it for himself. Did you hear him say he drank the first? He claimed to be the best by drinking first.

ANOTHER.

Did Cuchulain drink the first?

LAEG [*triumphantly*].

You drank the first, Cuchulain.

CONAL.

Did you claim to be better than us by drinking first?

[LEAGERIE *and* CONAL *draw their swords.*

CUCHULAIN.

Is it that old dried herring, that old red juggler who has made us quarrel for his own comfort? [*The* Horseboys *and the* Scullions *murmur excitedly.*] He gave the Helmet to set us by the ears, and because we would not quarrel over it, he goes to Laeg and tells him that I am wronged. Who knows where he is now, or who he is stirring up to make mischief between us? Go back to your work and do not stir from it whatever noise comes to you or whatever shape shows itself.

A SCULLION.

Cuchulain is right.   I am tired blowing on
the big horn.

CUCHULAIN.

Go in silence.

[*The* Scullions *and* Horseboys *turn towards
the door, but stand still on hearing the voice
of* LEAGERIE'S WIFE *outside the door.*

LEAGERIE'S WIFE.

My man is the best.   I will go in the first.
I will go in the first.

EMER.

My man is the best, and I will go in first.

CONAL'S WIFE.

No, for my man is the best, and it is I that
should go first.

[LEAGERIE'S WIFE *and* CONAL'S WIFE *struggle
in the doorway.*

LEAGERIE'S WIFE *sings.*

My man is the best.
What other has fought
The cat-headed men
That mew in the sea
And carried away
Their long-hidden gold?
They struck with their claws
And bit with their teeth,
But Leagerie my husband
Put all to the sword.

CONAL'S WIFE.

[*Putting her hand over the other's mouth
and getting in front of her.*]

My husband has fought
With strong men in armour.
Had he a quarrel
With cats, it is certain
He'd war with none
But the stout and heavy
With good claws on them.
What glory in warring
With hollow shadows
That helplessly mew?

EMER.

[*Thrusting herself between them and forcing
both of them back with her hands.*]

I am Emer, wife of Cuchulain, and no one
shall go in front of me, or sing in front of me, or
praise any that I have not a mind to hear praised.

[CUCHULAIN *puts his spear across the door.*

CUCHULAIN.

All of our three wives shall come in to-
gether, and by three doors equal in height
and in breadth and in honour. Break down
the bottoms of the windows.

[*While* CONAL *and* LEAGERIE *are breaking down
the bottoms of the windows each of their wives
goes to the window where her husband is.*

While the windows are being broken down
EMER *sings.*

My man is the best.
And Conal's wife
And the wife of Leagerie
Know that they lie
When they praise their own
Out of envy of me.
My man is the best,
First for his own sake,
Being the bravest
And handsomest man
And the most beloved
By the women of Ireland
That envy me,
And then for his wife's sake
Because I'm the youngest
And handsomest queen.

[*When the windows have been made into doors,*
CUCHULAIN *takes his spear from the door
where* EMER *is, and all three come in at the
same moment.*

EMER.

I am come to praise you and to put courage
into you, Cuchulain, as a wife should, that they
may not take the championship of the men of
Ireland from you.

LEAGERIE'S WIFE.

You lie, Emer, for it is Cuchulain and Conal who are taking the championship from my husband.

CONAL'S WIFE.

Cuchulain has taken it.

CUCHULAIN.

Townland against townland, barony against barony, kingdom against kingdom, province against province, and if there be but two door-posts to a door the one fighting against the other. [*He takes up the Helmet which* LEAGERIE *had laid down upon the table when he went to break out the bottom of the window.*] This Helmet will bring no more wars into Ireland. [*He throws it into the sea.*]

LEAGERIE'S WIFE.

You have done that to rob my husband.

CONAL'S WIFE.

You could not keep it for yourself, and so you threw it away that nobody else might have it.

CONAL.

You should not have done that, Cuchulain.

LEAGERIE.

You have done us a great wrong.

EMER.

Who is for Cuchulain?

CUCHULAIN.

Let no one stir.

EMER.

Who is for Cuchulain, I say?

[*She draws her dagger from her belt and sings the same words as before, flourishing it about. While she has been singing,* CONAL'S WIFE *and* LEAGERIE'S WIFE *have drawn their daggers and run at her to kill her, but* CUCHULAIN *has forced them back.* CONAL *and* LEAGERIE *have drawn their swords to strike* CUCHULAIN.

CONAL'S WIFE.

[*While* EMER *is still singing.*]

Silence her voice, silence her voice, blow the horns, make a noise!

[*The* Scullions *and* Horseboys *blow their horns or fight among themselves. There is a deafening noise and a confused fight. Suddenly three black hands holding extinguishers come through the window and extinguish the torches. It is now pitch dark but for a very faint light outside the house which merely shows that there are moving forms, but not who or what they are, and in the darkness one can hear low terrified voices.*

FIRST VOICE.

Did you see them putting out the torches?

ANOTHER VOICE.

They came up out of the sea, three black men.

ANOTHER VOICE.

They have heads of cats upon them.

ANOTHER VOICE.

They came up mewing out of the sea.

ANOTHER VOICE.

How dark it is! one of them has put his hand over the moon.

[*A light gradually comes into the windows as if shining from the sea. The* RED MAN *is seen standing in the midst of the house.*

RED MAN.

I demand the debt that is owing. I demand that some man shall stoop down that I may cut his head off as my head was cut off. If my debt is not paid, no peace shall come to Ireland, and Ireland shall lie weak before her enemies. But if my debt is paid there shall be peace.

CUCHULAIN.

The quarrels of Ireland shall end. What is one man's life? I will pay the debt with my own head. [EMER *wails.*] Do not cry out, Emer, for if I were not myself, if I were not Cuchulain,

one of those that God has made reckless, the
women of Ireland had not loved me, and you
had not held your head so high. [*He stoops,
bending his head. Three* Black Men *come to the
door. Two hold torches, and one stooping between
them holds up the Golden Helmet. The* RED MAN
gives one of the Black Men *his sword and takes the
Helmet.*] What do you wait for, old man?
Come, raise up your sword!

RED MAN.

I will not harm you, Cuchulain. I am the
guardian of this land, and age after age I come
up out of the sea to try the men of Ireland. I
give you the championship because you are
without fear, and you shall win many battles
with laughing lips and endure wounding and
betrayal without bitterness of heart; and when
men gaze upon you, their hearts shall grow
greater and their minds clear; until the day
come when I darken your mind, that there
may be an end to the story, and a song on the
harp-string.

The Irish dramatic movement began in May, 1899, with the performance of certain plays by English actors who were brought to Dublin for the purpose; and in the spring of the following year and in the autumn of the year after that, performances of like plays were given by like actors at the Gaiety Theatre, Dublin. In the third year I started SAMHAIN *to defend the work, and on re-reading it and reading it for the first time throughout, have found it best to reprint my part of it unchanged. A number has been published about once a year till very lately, and the whole series of notes are a history of a movement which is important because of the principles it is rooted in whatever be its fruits, and these principles are better told of in words that rose out of the need, than were I to explain all again and with order and ceremony now that the old enmities and friendships are ruffled by new ones that have other things to be done and said.*

March, 1908.

SAMHAIN: 1901

When Lady Gregory, Mr. Edward Martyn, and myself planned the Irish Literary Theatre, we decided that it should be carried on in the form we had projected for three years. We thought that three years would show whether the country desired to take up the project, and make it a part of the national life, and that we, at any rate, could return to our proper work, in which we did not include theatrical management, at the end of that time. A little later, Mr. George Moore* joined us; and, looking back now upon our work, I doubt if it could have been done at all without his knowledge of the stage; and certainly if the performances of this present year bring our adventure to a successful close, a chief part of the credit will be his. Many, however, have helped us in various degrees, for in Ireland just now one has only to discover an idea that seems of service to the country for friends and helpers to start up on every hand. While we needed guarantors we had them in plenty, and though Mr. Edward Martyn's public spirit made it unnecessary to call upon them, we thank them none the less.

* Both Mr. Moore and Mr. Martyn dropped out of the movement after the third performance at the Irish Literary Theatre in 1901.—W.B.Y.

Whether the Irish Literary Theatre has a successor made on its own model or not, we can claim that a dramatic movement which will not die has been started. When we began our work, we tried in vain to get a play in Gaelic. We could not even get a condensed version of the dialogue of Oisin and Patrick. We wrote to Gaelic enthusiasts in vain, for their imagination had not yet turned towards the stage, and now there are excellent Gaelic plays by Dr. Douglas Hyde, by Father O'Leary, by Father Dineen, and by Mr. MacGinlay; and the Gaelic League has had a competition for a one-act play in Gaelic, with what results I do not know. There have been successful performances of plays in Gaelic at Dublin and at Macroom, and at Letterkenny, and I think at other places; and Mr. Fay has got together an excellent little company which plays both in Gaelic and English. I may say, for I am perhaps writing an epitaph, and epitaphs should be written in a genial spirit, that we have turned a great deal of Irish imagination towards the stage. We could not have done this if our movement had not opened a way of expression for an impulse that was in the people themselves. The truth is that the Irish people are at that precise stage of their history when imagination, shaped by many stirring events, desires dramatic expression. One has only to listen to a recitation of Raftery's *Argument with Death* at some country Feis to understand this. When Death makes a good point, or Raftery a good point, the audience applaud delightedly, and applaud, not as a London audience would, some verbal dexterity, some piece of smartness, but the movements of a simple and fundamental comedy. One sees it too in the reciters themselves, whose acting is at times all but perfect in its vivid simplicity. I heard a little Claddagh girl tell a folk-story at Galway Feis with a restraint and a delightful energy that could hardly have been bettered by the most careful training.

The organization of this movement is of immediate importance. Some of our friends propose that somebody begin at once to get a small stock company together, and that he invite, let us say, Mr. Benson, to find us certain well-trained actors, Irish if possible, but well trained of a certainty, who will train our actors, and take the more difficult parts at the beginning. These friends contend that it is necessary to import our experts at the beginning, for our company must be able to compete with travelling English companies, but that a few years will be enough to make many competent Irish actors. The Corporation of Dublin should be asked, they say, to give a small annual sum of money, such as they give to the Academy of Music; and the Corporations of Cork and Limerick and Waterford, and other provincial towns, to give small endowments in the shape of a hall and attendants and lighting for a week or two out of every year; and the Technical Board to give a small annual sum of money to a school of acting which would teach fencing and declamation, and gesture and the like. The stock company would perform in Dublin perhaps three weeks in spring, and three weeks in autumn, and go on tour the rest of the time through Ireland, and through the English towns where there is a large Irish population. It would perform plays in Irish and English, and also, it is proposed, the masterpieces of the world, making a point of performing Spanish and Scandinavian, and French, and perhaps Greek masterpieces rather more than Shakespeare, for Shakespeare one sees, not well done indeed, but not unendurably ill done in the Theatre of Commerce. It would do its best to give Ireland a hardy and shapely national character by opening the doors to the four winds of the world, instead of leaving the door that is towards the east wind open alone. Certainly, the national character, which is so essentially different from the English that Spanish and French influences may well be most healthy, is at present like one of those miserable thorn bushes by the sea that are all twisted to one side by some prevailing wind.

It is contended that there is no reason why the company should not be as successful as similar companies in Germany and Scandinavia, and that it would be even of commercial advantage to Dublin by making it a pleasanter place to live in, besides doing incalculable good to the whole intellect of the country. One, at any rate, of those who press the project on us has much practical knowledge of the stage and of theatrical management, and knows what is possible and what is not possible.

Others among our friends, and among these are some who have had more than their share of the hard work which has built up the intellectual movement in Ireland, argue that a theatre of this kind would require too much money to be free, that it could not touch on politics, the most vital passion and vital

interest of the country, as they say, and that the atti-
tude of continual compromise between conviction and
interest, which it would necessitate, would become
demoralising to everybody concerned, especially at
moments of political excitement. They tell us that
the war between an Irish Ireland and an English Ire-
land is about to become much fiercer, to divide families
and friends it may be, and that the organisations that
will lead in the war must be able to say everything
the people are thinking. They would have Irishmen
give their plays to a company like Mr. Fay's, when
they are within its power, and if not, to Mr. Benson
or to any other travelling company which will play
them in Ireland without committees, where everybody
compromises a little. In this way, they contend, we
would soon build up an Irish theatre from the ground,
escaping to some extent the conventions of the or-
dinary theatre, and English voices which give a foreign
air to one's words. And though we might have to
wait some years, we would get even the masterpieces
of the world in good time. Let us, they think, be
poor enough to whistle at the thief who would take
away some of our thoughts, and after Mr. Fay has
taken his company, as he plans, through the villages
and the country towns, he will get the little endow-
ment that is necessary, or if he does not some other will.

I do not know what Lady Gregory or Mr. Moore
think of these projects. I am not going to say what I
think. I have spent much of my time and more of
my thought these last ten years on Irish organisation,
and now that the Irish Literary Theatre has completed
the plan I had in my head ten years ago, I want to

go down again to primary ideas. I want to put old stories into verse, and if I put them into dramatic verse it will matter less to me henceforward who plays them than what they play, and how they play. I hope to get our heroic age into verse, and to solve some problems of the speaking of verse to musical notes.

There is only one question which is raised by the two projects I have described on which I will give an opinion. It is of the first importance that those among us who want to write for the stage study the dramatic masterpieces of the world. If they can get them on the stage so much the better, but study them they must if Irish drama is to mean anything to Irish intellect. At the present moment, Shakespeare being the only great dramatist known to Irish writers has made them cast their work too much on the English model. Miss Milligan's *Red Hugh*, which was successfully acted in Dublin the other day, had no business to be in two scenes; and Father O'Leary's *Tadg Saor*, despite its most vivid and picturesque, though far too rambling dialogue, shows in its half dozen changes of scene the influence of the same English convention which arose when there was no scene painting, and is often a difficulty where there is, and is always an absurdity in a farce of thirty minutes, breaking up the emotion and sending one's thoughts here and there. Mr. MacGinlay's *Elis agus an bhean deirce* has not this defect, and though I had not Irish enough to follow it when I saw it played, and excellently played, by Mr. Fay's company, I could see from the continual laughter of the audience that it held them with an unbroken emotion. The best Gaelic play after Dr.

Hyde's is, I think, Father Dineen's *Creideamh agus gorta*, and though it changes the scene a little oftener than is desirable under modern conditions, it does not remind me of an English model. It reminds me of Calderon by its treatment of a religious subject, and by something in Father Dineen's sympathy with the people that is like his. But I think if Father Dineen had studied that great Catholic dramatist he would not have failed, as he has done once or twice, to remember some necessary detail of a situation. In the first scene he makes a servant ask his fellow-servants about things he must have known as well as they; and he loses a dramatic moment in his third scene by forgetting that Seagan Gorm has a pocket-full of money which he would certainly, being the man he was, have offered to the woman he was urging into temptation. The play towards the end changes from prose to verse, and the reverence and simplicity of the verse makes one think of a mediæval miracle play. The subject has been so much a part of Irish life that it was bound to be used by an Irish dramatist, though certainly I shall always prefer plays which attack a more eternal devil than the proselytiser. He has been defeated, and the arts are at their best when they are busy with battles that can never be won. It is possible, however, that we may have to deal with passing issues until we have re-created the imaginative tradition of Ireland, and filled the popular imagination again with saints and heroes. These short plays (though they would be better if their writers knew the masters of their craft) are very dramatic as they are, but there is no chance of our writers of Gaelic, or our writers of English, doing good plays of any length if

they do not study the masters. If Irish dramatists had
studied the romantic plays of Ibsen, the one great
master the modern stage has produced, they would
not have sent the Irish Literary Theatre imitations
of Boucicault, who had no relation to literature, and
Father O'Leary would have put his gift for dialogue,
a gift certainly greater than, let us say, Mr. Jones' or
Mr. Grundy's, to better use than the writing of that
long rambling dramatisation of the *Tain bo Cuailgne*,
in which I hear in the midst of the exuberant Gaelic
dialogue the worn-out conventions of English poetic
drama. The moment we leave even a little the folk-
tradition of the peasant, as we must in drama, if we
do not know the best that has been said and written
in the world, we do not even know ourselves. It is
no great labour to know the best dramatic literature,
for there is very little of it. We Irish must know it
all, for we have, I think, far greater need of the severe
discipline of French and Scandinavian drama than of
Shakespeare's luxuriance.

If the *Diarmuid and Grania* and the *Casàdh an
t-Sugain* are not well constructed, it is not because
Mr. Moore and Dr. Hyde and myself do not under-
stand the importance of construction, and Mr.
Martyn has shown by the triumphant construction
of *The Heather Field* how much thought he has given
to the matter; but for the most part our Irish plays
read as if they were made without a plan, without a
'scenario,' as it is called. European drama began
so, but the European drama had centuries for its
growth, while our art must grow to perfection in a
generation or two if it is not to be smothered before it

is well above the earth by what is merely commercial
in the art of England.

Let us learn construction from the masters, and
dialogue from ourselves. A relation of mine has
just written me a letter, in which he says: 'It is
natural to an Irishman to write plays, he has an in-
born love of dialogue and sound about him, of a
dialogue as lively, gallant, and passionate as in the
times of great Eliza. In these days an Englishman's
dialogue is that of an amateur, that is to say, it is
never spontaneous. I mean in *real life*. Compare
it with an Irishman's, above all a poor Irishman's,
reckless abandonment and naturalness, or compare
it with the only fragment that has come down to us of
Shakespeare's own conversation.' (He is remember-
ing a passage in, I think, Ben Jonson's *Underwoods*.)
'Petty commerce and puritanism have brought to
the front the wrong type of Englishman ; the lively,
joyous, yet tenacious man has transferred himself to
Ireland. We have him and we will keep him unless
the combined nonsense of . . . and . . . and . . .
succeed in suffocating him.'

In Dublin the other day I saw a poster advertising
a play by a Miss . . . under the patronage of certain
titled people. I had little hope of finding any reality
in it, but I sat out two acts. Its dialogue was above
the average, though the characters were the old rattle-
traps of the stage, the wild Irish girl, and the Irish
servant, and the bowing Frenchman, and the situa-
tions had all been squeezed dry generations ago.
One saw everywhere the shadowy mind of a woman

of the Irish upper classes as they have become to-day, but under it all there was a kind of life, though it was but the life of a string and a wire. I do not know who Miss . . . is, but I know that she is young, for I saw her portrait in a weekly paper, and I think that she is clever enough to make her work of some importance. If she goes on doing bad work she will make money, perhaps a great deal of money, but she will do a little harm to her country. If, on the other hand, she gets into an original relation with life, she will, perhaps, make no money, and she will certainly have her class against her.

The Irish upper classes put everything into a money measure. When anyone among them begins to write or paint they ask him 'How much money have you made?' 'Will it pay?' Or they say, 'If you do this or that you will make more money.' The poor Irish clerk or shopboy,* who writes verses or articles in his brief leisure, writes for the glory of God and of his country; and because his motive is high, there is not one vulgar thought in the countless little ballad books that have been written from Callinan's day to this. They are often clumsily written for they are in English, and if you have not read a great deal, it is difficult to write well in a language which has been long separated, from the 'folk-speech'; but they have not a thought a proud and simple man would not have written. The writers were poor men, but they left that money measure to the Irish upper classes. All Irish writers have to choose whether they will write as the upper

* That mood has gone, with Fenianism and its wild hopes. The National movement has been commercialized in the last few years. How much real ideality is but hidden for a time one cannot say.—W.B.Y., *March*, 1908.

classes have done, not to express but to exploit this country; or join the intellectual movement which has raised the cry that was heard in Russia in the seventies, the cry 'to the people.'

Moses was little good to his people until he had killed an Egyptian; and for the most part a writer or public man of the upper classes is useless to this country till he has done something that separates him from his class. We wish to grow peaceful crops, but we must dig our furrows with the sword.

Our plays this year will be produced by Mr. Benson at the Gaiety Theatre on October the 21st, and on some of the succeeding days. They are Dr. Douglas Hyde's *Casadh an t-Sugain*, which is founded on a well known Irish story of a wandering poet; and *Diarmuid and Grania*, a play in three acts and in prose by Mr. George Moore and myself, which is founded on the most famous of all Irish stories, the story of the lovers whose beds were the cromlechs. The first act of *Diarmuid and Grania* is in the great banqueting hall of Tara, and the second and third on the slopes of Ben Bulben in Sligo. We do not think there is anything in either play to offend anybody, but we make no promises. We thought our plays inoffensive last year and the year before, but we were accused the one year of sedition, and the other of heresy.

I have called this little collection of writings *Samhain*, the old name for the beginning of winter, because our plays this year are in October, and because our Theatre is coming to an end in its present shape.

1902

The Irish Literary Theatre wound up its three
years of experiment last October with *Diarmuid and
Grania,* which was played by Mr. Benson's Company,
Mr. Benson himself playing Diarmuid with poetry
and fervour, and *Casadh an t-Sugain,* played by Dr.
Hyde and some members of the Gaelic League.
Diarmuid and Grania drew large audiences, but its
version of the legend was a good deal blamed by
critics, who knew only the modern text of the story.
There are two versions, and the play was fully jus-
tified by Irish and Scottish folk-lore, and by certain
early Irish texts, which do not see Grania through
very friendly eyes.   Any critic who is interested in
so dead a controversy can look at the folk-tales
quoted by Campbell in, I think, *West Highland Super-
stitions,* and at the fragment translated by Kuno
Meyer, at page 458 of Vol. I. of *Zeitschrift für Kelt-
ische Philologie.*   Dr. Hyde's play, on the other hand,
pleased everybody, and has been played a good many
times in a good many places since.   It was the first
play in Irish played in a theatre, and did much
towards making plays a necessary part in Irish pro-
paganda.

The Irish Literary Theatre has given place to a
company of Irish actors.   Its Committee saw them
take up the work all the more gladly because it had
not formed them or influenced them.   A dramatic
society with guarantors and patrons can never have
more than a passing use, because it can never be

quite free ; and it is not successful until it is able to say it is no longer wanted. Amateur actors will perform for *Cumann-na-Gael* plays chosen by themselves, and written by A.E., by Mr. Cousins, by Mr. Ryan, by Mr. MacGinlay and by myself. These plays will be given at the Antient Concert Rooms at the end of October, but the National Theatrical Company will repeat their successes with new work in a very little hall they have hired in Camden Street. If they could afford it they would have hired some bigger house, but, after all, M. Antoine founded his *Théâtre Libre* with a company of amateurs in a hall that only held three hundred people.

The first work of theirs to get much attention was their performance, last spring, at the invitation of *Inghinidhe h-Eireann* of A.E.'s *Deirdre,* and my *Cathleen ni Houlihan.* They had Miss Maud Gonne's help, and it was a fine thing for so beautiful a woman to consent to play my poor old Cathleen, and she played with nobility and tragic power. She showed herself as good in tragedy as Dr. Hyde is in comedy, and stirred a large audience very greatly. The whole company played well, too, but it was in *Deirdre* that they interested me most. They showed plenty of inexperience, especially in the minor characters, but it was the first performance I had seen since I understood these things in which the actors kept still enough to give poetical writing its full effect upon the stage. I had imagined such acting, though I had not seen it, and had once asked a dramatic company to let me rehearse them in barrels that they might forget gesture and have their minds free to think of speech for a while. The barrels, I thought, might be on castors, so that I could shove them about with a pole when the action required it.   The other day I saw Sara Bernhardt and De Max in *Phèdre*, and understood where Mr. Fay, who stage-manages the National Theatrical Company, had gone for his model.* For long periods the performers would merely stand and pose, and I once counted twenty-seven quite slowly before anybody on a fairly well-filled stage moved, as it seemed, so much as an eye-lash. The periods of stillness were generally shorter, but I frequently counted seventeen, eighteen or twenty before there was a movement. I noticed, too, that the gestures had a rhythmic progression. Sara Bernhardt would keep her hands clasped over, let us say, her right breast for some time, and then move them to the other side, perhaps, lowering her chin till it touched her hands, and then, after another long stillness, she would unclasp them and hold one out, and so on, not lowering them till she had exhausted all the gestures of uplifted hands. Through one long scene De Max, who was quite as fine, never lifted his hand above his elbow, and it was only when the emotion came to its climax that he raised it to his breast.   Beyond them stood a crowd of white-robed men who never moved at all, and the whole scene had the nobility of Greek sculpture, and an extraordinary reality and intensity.   It was the most beautiful thing I had ever seen upon the stage, and made me understand, in a new way, that saying of Goethe's which is understood everywhere but in

* An illusion, as he himself explained to me. He had never seen *Phèdre*. The players were quiet and natural, because they did not know what else to do. They had not learned to go wrong.—W.B.Y., *March*, 1908.

England, 'Art is art because it is not nature.' Of course, our amateurs were poor and crude beside those great actors, perhaps the greatest in Europe, but they followed them as well as they could, and got an audience of artisans, for the most part, to admire them for doing it. I heard somebody who sat behind me say, 'They have got rid of all the nonsense.'

I thought the costumes and scenery, which were designed by A.E. himself, good, too, though I did not think them simple enough. They were more simple than ordinary stage costumes and scenery, but I would like to see poetical drama, which tries to keep at a distance from daily life that it may keep its emotion untroubled, staged with but two or three colours. The background, especially in small theatres, where its form is broken up and lost when the stage is at all crowded, should, I think, be thought out as one thinks out the background of a portrait. One often needs nothing more than a single colour with perhaps a few shadowy forms to suggest wood or mountain. Even on a large stage one should leave the description of the poet free to call up the martlet's procreant cradle or what he will. But I have written enough about decorative scenery elsewhere, and will probably lecture on that and like matters before we begin the winter's work.

The performances of *Deirdre* and *Cathleen ni Houlihan*, which will be repeated in the Antient Concert Rooms, drew so many to hear them that great numbers were turned away from the doors of

St. Theresa's Hall. Like the plays of the Irish
Literary Theatre, they started unexpected discussion.
Mr. Standish O'Grady, who had done more than any
other to make us know the old legends, wrote in his
All Ireland Review that old legends could not be staged
without danger of 'banishing the soul of the land.'
The old Irish had many wives for instance, and one
had best leave their histories to the vagueness of
legend. How could uneducated people understand
heroes who lived amid such different circumstances?
And so we were to 'leave heroic cycles alone, and
not to bring them down to the crowd.' A.E. replied
in the *United Irishman* with an impassioned letter.
'The old, forgotten music' he writes about in his
letter is, I think, that regulated music of speech at
which both he and I have been working, though on
somewhat different principles. I have been working
with Miss Farr and Mr. Arnold Dolmetsch, who has
made a psaltery for the purpose, to perfect a music
of speech which can be recorded in something like
ordinary musical notes; while A.E. has got a musician
to record little chants with intervals much smaller
than those of modern music.

After the production of these plays the most im-
portant Irish dramatic event was, no doubt, the acting
of Dr. Hyde's *An Posadh*, in Galway. Through an
accident it had been very badly rehearsed, but his own
acting made amends. One could hardly have had a
play that grew more out of the life of the people who
saw it. There may have been old men in that audi-
ence who remembered its hero the poet Raftery, and
there was nobody there who had not come from

hearing his poems repeated at the Galway Feis. I
think from its effect upon the audience that this play
in which the chief Gaelic poet of our time celebrates
his forerunner in simplicity, will be better liked in
Connaught at any rate than even *Casadh an t-Sugain.*
His *Tincear agus Sidheog,* acted in Mr. Moore's garden,
at the time of the Oireachtas, is a very good play, but
is, I think, the least interesting of his plays as liter-
ature. His imagination, which is essentially the folk-
imagination, needs a looser construction, and probably
a more crowded stage. A play that gets its effect by
keeping close to one idea reminds one, when it comes
from the hands of a folk-poet, of Blake's saying, that
'Improvement makes straight roads, but the crooked
roads are the roads of genius.' The idea loses the
richness of its own life, while it destroys the wayward
life of his mind by bringing it under too stern a law.
Nor could charming verses make amends for that
second kiss in which there was profanation, and for
that abounding black bottle. Did not M. Trebulet
Bonhommie discover that one spot of ink would kill
a swan ?

Among the other plays in Irish acted during the
year Father Dineen's *Tobar Draoidheachta* is probably
the best. He has given up the many scenes of his
Creadeamh agus Gorta, and has written a play in one
scene, which, as it can be staged without much trouble,
has already been played in several places. One
admires its *naïveté* as much as anything else. Father
Dineen, who, no doubt, remembers how Finn mac
Cumhal when a child was put in a field to catch hares
and keep him out of mischief, has sent the rival lovers

H

of his play when he wanted them off the scene for a moment, to catch a hare that has crossed the stage. When they return the good lover is carrying it by the heels, and modestly compares it to a lame jackass. One rather likes this bit of nonsense when one comes to it, for in that world of folk-imagination one thing seems as possible as another. On the other hand, there is a moment of beautiful dramatic tact. The lover gets a letter telling of the death of a relative in America, for whom he has no particular affection, and who has left him a fortune. He cannot lament, for that would be insincere, and his first words must not be rejoicing. Father Dineen has found for him the one beautiful thing he could say, 'It's a lonesome thing death is.' With, perhaps, less beauty than there is in the closing scene of *Creadeamh agus Gorta*, the play has more fancy and a more sustained energy.

Father Peter O'Leary has written a play in his usual number of scenes which has not been published, but has been acted amid much Munster enthusiasm. But neither that or *La an Amadan*, which has also been acted, are likely to have any long life on our country stages. A short play, with many changes of scene, is a nuisance in any theatre, and often an impossibility on our poor little stages. Some kind of play, in English, by Mr. Standish O'Grady, has been acted in the open air in Kilkenny. I have not seen it, and I cannot understand anything by the accounts of it, except that there were magic lantern slides and actors on horseback, and Mr. Standish O'Grady as an Elizabethan night-watchman, speaking prologues, and a contented audience of two or three thousand people.

As we do not think that a play can be worth acting and not worth reading, all our plays will be published in time. Some have been printed in *The United Irishman* and *The All Ireland Review*. I have put my *Cathleen ni Houlihan* and a little play by Dr. Hyde into this *Samhain*. Once already this year I have had what somebody has called the noble pleasure of praising, and I can praise this *Lost Saint* with as good a conscience as I had when I wrote of *Cuchulain of Muirthemne*. I would always admire it, but just now, when I have been thinking that literature should return to its old habit of describing desirable things, I am in the mood to be stirred by that old man gathering up food for fowl with his heart full of love, and by those children who are so full of the light-hearted curiosity of childhood, and by that schoolmaster who has mixed prayer with his gentle punishments. It seems natural that so beautiful a prayer as that of the old saint should have come out of a life so full of innocence and peace. One could hardly have thought out the play in English, for those phrases of a traditional simplicity and of a too deliberate prettiness which become part of an old language would have arisen between the mind and the story. One might even have made something as unreal as the sentimental schoolmaster of the Scottish novelists, and how many children, who are but literary images, would one not have had to hunt out of one's mind before meeting with those little children? Even if one could have thought it out in English one could not have written it in English, unless perhaps in that dialect which Dr. Hyde had already used in the prose narrative that flows about his *Love Songs of Connaught*.

Dr. Hyde has written a little play about the birth of Christ which has the same beauty and simplicity. These plays remind me of my first reading of *The Love Songs of Connaught*. The prose parts of that book were to me, as they were to many others, the coming of a new power into literature. I find myself now, as I found myself then, grudging to propaganda, to scholarship, to oratory, however necessary, a genius which might in modern Irish or in that idiom of the English-speaking country people discover a new region for the mind to wander in. In Ireland, where we have so much to prove and to disprove, we are ready to forget that the creation of an emotion of beauty is the only kind of literature that justifies itself. Books of literary propaganda and literary history are merely preparations for the creation or understanding of such an emotion. It is necessary to put so much in order, to clear away so much, to explain so much, that somebody may be moved by a thought or an image that is inexplicable as a wild creature.

I cannot judge the language of his Irish poetry, but it is so rich in poetical thought, when at its best, that it seems to me that if he were to write more he might become to modern Irish what Mistral was to modern Provençal. I wish, too, that he could put away from himself some of the interruptions of that ceaseless propaganda, and find time for the making of translations, loving and leisurely, like those in *Beside the Fire* and *The Love Songs of Connaught*. He has begun to get a little careless lately. Above all I would have him keep to that English idiom of the Irish-thinking people of the west which he has begun

to use less often. It is the only good English spoken
by any large number of Irish people to-day, and one
must found good literature on a living speech.
English men of letters found themselves upon the
English Bible, where religious thought gets its living
speech. Blake, if I remember rightly, copied it out
twice, and I remember once finding a few illuminated
pages of a new decorated copy that he began in his
old age. Byron read it for the sake of style, though
I think it did him little good, and Ruskin founded
himself in great part upon it. Indeed, one finds every-
where signs of a book which is the chief influence in
the lives of English children. The translation used
in Ireland has not the same literary beauty, and if we
are to find anything to take its place we must find it
in that idiom of the poor, which mingles so much of
the same vocabulary with turns of phrase that have
come out of Gaelic. Even Irish writers of consider-
able powers of thought seem to have no better
standard of English than a schoolmaster's ideal of
correctness. If their grammar is correct they will
write in all the lightness of their hearts about 'keeping
in touch,' and 'object-lessons,' and 'shining examples,'
and 'running in grooves,' and 'flagrant violations' of
various things. Yet, as Sainte-Beuve has said, there is
nothing immortal except style. One can write well in
that country idiom without much thought about one's
words, the emotion will bring the right word itself,
for there everything is old and everything alive and
nothing common or threadbare. I recommend to the
Intermediate Board—a body that seems to benefit by
advice—a better plan than any they know for teach-
ing children to write good English. Let every child

in Ireland be set to turn a leading article or a piece
of what is called excellent English, written perhaps
by some distinguished member of the Board, into the
idiom of his own country side. He will find at once
the difference between dead and living words, between
words that meant something years ago, and words that
have the only thing that gives literary quality—per-
sonality, the breath of men's mouths. Zola, who is
sometimes an admirable critic, has said that some of
the greatest pages in French literature are not even
right in their grammar, 'They are great because they
have personality.'

The habit of writing for the stage, even when it is
not country people who are the speakers, and of con-
sidering what good dialogue is, will help to increase
our feeling for style. Let us get back in everything
to the spoken word, even though we have to speak
our lyrics to the Psaltery or the Harp, for, as A.E.
says, we have begun to forget that literature is but
recorded speech, and even when we write with care
we have begun 'to write with elaboration what could
never be spoken.' But when we go back to speech
let us see that it is either the idiom of those who
have rejected, or of those who have never learned,
the base idioms of the newspapers.

Mr. Martyn argued in *The United Irishman* some
months ago that our actors should try to train them-
selves for the modern drama of society. The acting of
plays of heroic life or plays like *Cathleen ni Houlihan*,
with its speech of the country people, did not seem
to him a preparation. It is not; but that is as it should
be. Our movement is a return to the people, like

the Russian movement of the early seventies, and the drama of society would but magnify a condition of life which the countryman and the artisan could but copy to their hurt. The play that is to give them a quite natural pleasure should either tell them of their own life, or of that life of poetry where every man can see his own image, because there alone does human nature escape from arbitrary conditions. Plays about drawing-rooms are written for the middle classes of great cities, for the classes who live in drawing-rooms, but if you would uplift the man of the roads you must write about the roads, or about the people of romance, or about great historical people. We should, of course, play every kind of good play about Ireland that we can get, but romantic and historical plays, and plays about the life of artisans and country people are the best worth getting. In time, I think, we can make the poetical play a living dramatic form again, and the training our actors will get from plays of country life, with its unchanging outline, its abundant speech, its extravagance of thought, will help to establish a school of imaginative acting. The play of society, on the other hand, could but train up realistic actors who would do badly, for the most part, what English actors do well, and would, when at all good, drift away to wealthy English theatres. If, on the other hand, we busy ourselves with poetry and the countryman, two things which have always mixed with one another in life as on the stage, we may recover, in the course of years, a lost art which, being an imitation of nothing English, may bring our actors a secure fame and a sufficient livelihood.

1903

I CANNOT describe the various dramatic adventures
of the year with as much detail as I did last year,
mainly because the movement has got beyond me.
The most important event of the Gaelic Theatre has
been the two series of plays produced in the Round
Room of the Rotunda by the Gaelic League. Father
Dineen's *Tobar Draoidheachta*, and Dr. Hyde's *An
Posadh*, and a chronicle play about Hugh O'Neill,
and, I think, some other plays, were seen by immense
audiences. I was not in Ireland for these plays, but
a friend tells me that he could only get standing-room
one night, and the Round Room must hold about
3,000 people. A performance of *Tobar Draoidheachta*
I saw there some months before, was bad, but I be-
lieve there was great improvement, and that the
players who came up from somewhere in County Cork
to play it at this second series of plays were admir-
able. The players, too, that brought Dr. Hyde's *An
Posadh* from Ballaghadereen, in County Mayo, where
they had been showing it to their neighbours, were
also, I am told, careful and natural. The play-writing,
always good in dialogue, is still very poor in con-
struction, and I still hear of plays in many scenes,
with no scene lasting longer than four or six minutes,
and few intervals shorter than nine or ten minutes,
which have to be filled up with songs. The Rotunda
chronicle play seems to have been rather of this sort,
and I suspect that when I get Father Peter O'Leary's
Meadhbh, a play in five acts produced at Cork, I shall
find the masterful old man, in spite of his hatred of

English thought, sticking to the Elizabethan form. I wish I could have seen it played last week, for the spread of the Gaelic Theatre in the country is more important than its spread in Dublin, and of all the performances in Gaelic plays in the country during the year I have seen but one—Dr. Hyde's new play, *Cleamhnas*, at Galway Feis. I got there a day late for a play by the Master of Galway Workhouse, but heard that it was well played, and that his dialogue was as good as his construction was bad. There is no question, however, about the performance of *Cleamhnas* being the ·worst I ever saw. I do not blame the acting, which was pleasant and natural, in spite of insufficient rehearsal, but the stage-management. The subject of the play was a match-making. The terms were in debate between two old men in an inner room. An old woman, according to the stage directions, should have listened at the door and reported what she heard to her daughter's suitor, who is outside the window, and to her daughter. There was no window on the stage, and the young man stood close enough to the door to have listened for himself. The door, where she listened, opened now on the inner room, and now on the street, according to the necessities of the play, and the young men who acted the fathers of grown-up children, when they came through the door were seen to have done nothing to disguise their twenty-five or twenty-six birthdays. There had been only two rehearsals, and the little boy who should have come in laughing at the end came in shouting, 'Ho ho, ha ha,' evidently believing that these were Gaelic words he had never heard before. Playwrights will have to be careful who they permit to play their work if it is to be played after only two rehearsals, and without enough attention to the arrangement of the stage to make the action plausible.

The only Gaelic performances I have seen during the year have been ill-done, but I have seen them sufficiently well done in other years to believe my friends when they tell me that there have been good performances. *Inghinidhe na h-Eireann* is always thorough, and one cannot doubt that the performance of Dr. Hyde's *An Naom ar Iarriad*, by the children from its classes, was at least careful. A powerful little play in English against enlisting, by Mr. Colum, was played with it, and afterwards revived, and played with a play about the Royal Visit, also in English. I have no doubt that we shall see a good many of these political plays during the next two or three years, and it may be even the rise of a more or less permanent company of political players, for the revolutionary clubs will begin to think plays as necessary as the Gaelic League is already thinking them. Nobody can find the same patriotic songs and recitations sung and spoken by the same people, year in year out, anything but mouldy bread. It is possible that the players who are to produce plays in October for the Samhain festival of *Cumann na n-Gaedheal* may grow into such a company.

Though one welcomes every kind of vigorous life, I am, myself, most interested in 'The Irish National Theatre Society,' which has no propaganda but that of good art. The little Camden Street Hall it had

taken has been useful for rehearsal alone, for it proved
to be too far away, and too lacking in dressing-rooms
for our short plays, which involve so many changes.
Successful performances were given, however, at
Rathmines, and in one or two country places./

Deirdre, by A.E., *The Racing Lug*, by Mr. Cousins,
The Foundations, by Mr. Ryan, and my *Pot of Broth*,
and *Cathleen ni Houlihan*, were repeated, but no new
plays were produced until March 14th, when Lady
Gregory's *Twenty-five* and my *Hour-Glass*, drew a
good audience. On May 2nd the *Hour-Glass*, *Twenty-
five*, *Cathleen ni Houlihan*, *Pot of Broth*, and *Founda-
tions* were performed before the Irish Literary Society
in London, at the Queen's Gate Hall, and plays and
players were generously commended by the Press—
very eloquently by the critic of *The Times*. It is
natural that we should be pleased with this praise,
and that we should wish others to know of it, for is it
not a chief pleasure of the artist to be commended in
subtle and eloquent words? The critic of *The Times*
has seen many theatres and he is, perhaps, a little
weary of them, but here in Ireland there are one or
two critics who are so much in love, or pretend to be
so much in love, with the theatre as it is, that they
complain when we perform on a stage two feet wider
than Molière's that it is scarce possible to be in-
terested in anything that is played on so little a stage.
We are to them foolish sectaries who have revolted
against that orthodoxy of the commercial theatre,
which is so much less pliant than the orthodoxy of
the church, for there is nothing so passionate as a·
vested interest disguised as an intellectual conviction.

If you inquire into its truth it becomes as angry as a begging-letter writer, when you find some hole in that beautiful story about the five children and the broken mangle. In Ireland, wherever the enthusiasts are shaping life, the critic who does the will of the commercial theatre can but stand against his lonely pillar defending his articles of belief among a wild people, and thinking mournfully of distant cities, where nobody puts a raw potato into his pocket when he is going to hear a musical comedy.

The *Irish Literary Society* of New York, which has been founded this year, produced *The Land of Heart's Desire*, *The Pot of Broth*, and *Cathleen ni Houlihan*, on June 3rd and 4th, very successfully, and propose to give Dr. Hyde's Nativity Play, *Drama Breithe Chriosta*, and his *Casadh an t-Sugain*, *Posadh* and *Naom ar Iarriad* next year, at the same time of year, playing them both in Irish and English. I heard too that his Nativity Play will be performed in New York this winter, but I know no particulars except that it will be done in connection with some religious societies. *The National Theatre Society* will, I hope, produce some new plays of his this winter, as well as new plays by Mr. Synge, Mr. Colum, Lady Gregory, myself, and others. They have taken the Molesworth Hall for three days in every month, beginning with the 8th, 9th, and 10th of October, when they will perform Mr. Synge's *Shadow of the Glen*, a little country comedy, full of a humour that is at once harsh and beautiful, *Cathleen ni Houlihan*, and a longish one-act play in verse of my own, called *The King's Threshold*. .This play is founded on the old story of

Seanchan the poet, and King Guaire of Gort, but I have seen the story from the poet's point of view, and not, like the old storytellers, from the king's. Our repertory of plays is increasing steadily, and when the winter's work is finished, a play* Mr. Bernard Shaw has promised us may be ready to open the summer session. His play will, I imagine, unlike the plays we write for ourselves, be long enough to fill an evening, and it will, I know, deal with Irish public life and character. Mr. Shaw, more than anybody else, has the love of mischief that is so near the core of Irish intellect, and should have an immense popularity among us. I have seen a crowd of many thousands in possession of ·his spirit, and keeping the possession to the small hours.

This movement should be important even to those who are not especially interested in the Theatre, for it may be a morning cock-crow to that impartial meditation about character and destiny we call the artistic life in a country where everybody, if we leave out the peasant who has his folk-songs and his music, has thought the arts useless unless they have helped some kind of political action, and has, therefore, lacked the pure joy that only comes out of things that have never been indentured to any cause. The play which is mere propaganda shows its leanness more obviously than a propagandist poem or essay, for dramatic writing is so full of the stuff of daily life that a little falsehood, put in that the moral

* This play was *John Bull's Other Island.* When it came out in the spring of 1905 we felt ourselves unable to cast it without wronging Mr. Shaw. We had no 'Broadbent' or money to get one.—W.B.Y., *March,* 1908.

may come right in the end, contradicts our experience. If Father Dineen or Dr. Hyde were asked why they write their plays, they would say they write them to help their propaganda; and yet when they begin to write the form constrains them, and they become artists—one of them a very considerable artist, indeed. Dr. Hyde's early poems have even in translation a *naïveté* and wildness that sets them, as I think, among the finest poetry of our time; but he had ceased to write any verses but those Oireachtas odes that are but ingenious rhetoric. It is hard to write without the sympathy of one's friends, and though the country people sang his verses the readers of Irish read them but little, partly it may be because he had broken with that elaborate structure of later Irish poetry which seemed a necessary part of their propaganda. They read plenty of pamphlets and grammars, but they disliked—as do other people in Ireland—serious reading, reading that is an end and not a means, that gives us nothing but a beauty indifferent to our profuse purposes. But now Dr. Hyde with his cursing Hanrahan, his old saint at his prayers, is a poet again; and the Leaguers go to his plays in thousands —and applaud in the right places, too—and the League puts many sixpences into its pocket.

We who write in English have a more difficult work, for English has been the language in which the Irish cause has been debated; and we have to struggle with traditional phrases and traditional points of view. Many would give us limitless freedom as to the choice of subject, understanding that it is precisely those subjects on which people feel most passionately, and,

therefore, most dramatically, we would be forbidden
to handle if we made any compromise with powers.
But fewer know that we must encourage every writer
to see life afresh, even though he sees it with strange
eyes. Our National Theatre must be so tolerant, and,
if this is not too wild a hope, find an audience so
tolerant that the half-dozen minds, who are likely to
be the dramatic imagination of Ireland for this gene-
ration, may put their own thoughts and their own
characters into their work; and for that reason no
one who loves the arts, whether among Unionists or
among the Patriotic Societies, should take offence if
we refuse all but every kind of patronage. I do not
say every kind, for if a mad king, a king so mad that
he loved the arts and their freedom, should offer us
unconditioned millions, I, at any rate, would give my
voice for accepting them.

We will be able to find conscientious playwrights
and players, for our young men have a power of
work, when they are interested in their work, one
does not look for outside a Latin nation, and if we
were certain of being granted this freedom we would
be certain that the work would grow to great impor-
tance. It is a supreme moment in the life of a nation
when it is able to turn now and again from its pre-
occupations, to delight in the capricious power of the
·artist as one delights in the movement of some wild
creature, but nobody can tell with certainty when that
moment is at hand.

The two plays in this year's *Samhain* represent the
two sides of the movement very well, and are both

written out of a deep knowledge of the life of the people. It should be unnecessary to praise Dr. Hyde's comedy,* that comes up out of the foundation of human life, but Mr. Synge is a new writer and a creation of our movement. He has gone every summer for some years past to the Arran Islands, and lived there in the houses of the fishers, speaking their language and living their lives, and his play† seems to me the finest piece of tragic work done in Ireland of late years. One finds in it, from first to last, the presence of the sea, and a sorrow that has majesty as in the work of some ancient poet.

* *The Poor House*, written in Irish by Dr. Hyde on a scenario by Lady Gregory.
† *Riders to the Sea*. This play made its way very slowly with our audiences, but is now very popular.—W.B.Y., *March*, 1908.

THE REFORM OF THE THEATRE.

I think the theatre must be reformed in its plays, its speaking, its acting, and its scenery. That is to say, I think there is nothing good about it at present.

First. We have to write or find plays that will make the theatre a place of intellectual excitement—a place where the mind goes to be liberated as it was liberated by the theatres of Greece and England and France at certain great moments of their history, and as it is liberated in Scandinavia to-day. If we are to do this we must learn that beauty and truth are always justified of themselves, and that their creation is a greater service to our country than writing that compromises either in the seeming service of a cause. We will, doubtless, come more easily to truth and beauty because we love some cause with all but all our heart; but we must remember when truth and beauty open their mouths to speak, that all other mouths should be as silent as Finn bade the Son of Lugaidh be in the houses of the great. Truth and beauty judge and are above judgment. They justify and have no need of justification.

Such plays will require, both in writers and audiences, a stronger feeling for beautiful and appropriate language than one finds in the ordinary theatre. Sainte-Beuve has said that there is nothing immortal in literature except style, and it is precisely this sense of style, once common among us, that is hardest for us to recover. I do not mean by style words with an air of literature about them, what is ordinarily

I

called eloquent writing. The speeches of Falstaff are as perfect in their style as the soliloquies of Hamlet. One must be able to make a king of faery or an old countryman or a modern lover speak that language which is his and nobody else's, and speak it with so much of emotional subtlety that the hearer may find it hard to know whether it is the thought or the word that has moved him, or whether these could be separated at all.

If one does not know how to construct, if one cannot arrange much complicated life into a single action, one's work will not hold the attention or linger in the memory, but if one is not in love with words it will lack the delicate movement of living speech that is the chief garment of life; and because of this lack the great realists seem to the lovers of beautiful art to be wise in this generation, and for the next generation, perhaps, but not for all generations that are to come.

Second. But if we are to restore words to their sovereignty we must make speech even more important than gesture upon the stage.

I have been told that I desire a monotonous chant, but that is not true, for though a monotonous chant may be a safer beginning for an actor than the broken and prosaic speech of ordinary recitation, it puts one to sleep none the less. The sing-song in which a child says a verse is a right beginning, though the child grows out of it. An actor should understand how to so discriminate cadence from cadence, and to so cherish the musical lineaments of verse or prose that he delights the ear with a continually varied music. Certain passages of lyrical feeling, or where one wishes, as in the Angel's part in *The Hour-Glass*, to make a voice sound like the voice of an immortal, may be spoken upon pure notes which are carefully recorded and learned as if they were the notes of a song. Whatever method one adopts one must always be certain that the work of art, as a whole, is masculine and intellectual, in its sound as in its form.

Third. We must simplify acting, especially in poetical drama, and in prose drama that is remote from real life like my *Hour-Glass*. We must get rid of everything that is restless, everything that draws the attention away from the sound of the voice, or from the few moments of intense expression, whether that expression is through the voice or through the hands; we must from time to time substitute for the movements that the eye sees the nobler movements that the heart sees, the rhythmical movements that seem to flow up into the imagination from some deeper life than that of the individual soul.

Fourth. Just as it is necessary to simplify gesture that it may accompany speech without being its rival, it is necessary to simplify both the form and colour of scenery and costume. As a rule the background should be but a single colour, so that the persons in the play, wherever they stand, may harmonize with it and preoccupy our attention. In other words, it should be thought out not as one thinks out a landscape, but as if it were the background of a portrait, and this is especially necessary on a small stage where the moment the stage is filled the painted forms of the background are broken up and lost. Even when one has to represent trees or hills they should be treated in most cases decoratively, they should be

little more than an unobtrusive pattern. There must
be nothing unnecessary, nothing that will distract
the attention from speech and movement. An art is
always at its greatest when it is most human. Greek
acting was great because it did everything with the
voice, and modern acting may be great when it does
everything with voice and movement. But an art
which smothers these things with bad painting, with
innumerable garish colours, with continual restless
mimicries of the surface of life, is an art of fading
humanity, a decaying art.

MORAL AND IMMORAL PLAYS.

A writer in *The Leader* has said that I told my audience after the performance of *The Hour-Glass* that I did not care whether a play was moral or immoral. He said this without discourtesy, and as I have noticed that people are generally discourteous when they write about morals, I think that I owe him upon my part the courtesy of an explanation. I did not say that I did not care whether a play was moral or immoral, for I have always been of Verhaeren's opinion that a masterpiece is a portion of the conscience of mankind. My objection was to the rough-and-ready conscience of the newspaper and the pulpit in a matter so delicate and so difficult as literature. Every generation of men of letters has been called immoral by the pulpit or the newspaper, and it has been precisely when that generation has been illuminating some obscure corner of the conscience that the cry against it has been more confident.

The plays of Shakespeare had to be performed on the south side of the Thames because the Corporation of London considered all plays immoral. Goethe was thought dangerous to faith and morals for two or three generations. Every educated man knows how great a portion of the conscience of mankind is in Flaubert and Balzac, and yet their books have been proscribed in the courts of law, and I found some time ago that our own National Library, though it had two books on the genius of Flaubert, had refused on moral grounds to have any books written by him.

With these stupidities in one's memory, how can one, as many would have us, arouse the mob, and in this matter the pulpit and the newspaper are but voices of the mob, against the English theatre in Ireland upon moral grounds? If that theatre became conscientious as men of letters understand the conscience, many that now cry against it would think it even less moral, for it would be more daring, more logical, more free-spoken. The English Theatre is demoralizing, not because it delights in the husband, the wife and the lover, a subject which has inspired great literature in most ages of the world, but because the illogical thinking and insincere feeling we call bad writing, make the mind timid and the heart effeminate. I saw an English play in Dublin a few months ago called *Mice and Men*. It had run for five hundred nights in London, and been called by all the newspapers 'a pure and innocent play,' 'a welcome relief,' and so on. In it occurred this incident : The typical scapegrace hero of the stage, a young soldier, who is in love with the wife of another, goes away for a couple of years, and when he returns finds that he is in love with a marriageable girl. His mistress, who has awaited his return with what is represented as faithful love, sends him a letter of welcome, and because he has grown virtuous of a sudden he returns it unopened, and with so careless a scorn that the husband intercepts it ; and the dramatist approves this manner of crying off with an old love, and rings down the curtain on his marriage bells. Men who would turn such a man out of a club bring their wives and daughters to look at him with admiration upon the stage, so demoralizing is a drama that has no

intellectual tradition behind it. I could not endure it,
and went out into the street and waited there until
the end of the play, when I came in again to find the
friends I had brought to hear it, but had I been ac-
customed to the commercial theatre I would not even
have known that anything strange had happened upon
the stage. If a man of intellect had written of such an
incident he would have made his audience feel for the
mistress that sympathy one feels for all that have
suffered insult, and for that young man an ironical
emotion that might have marred the marriage bells,
and who knows what the curate and the journalist
would have said of him? Even Ireland would have
cried out: Catholic Ireland that should remember
the gracious tolerance of the Church when all nations
were its children, and how Wolfram of Eisenbach
sang from castle to castle of the courtesy of Parzival,
the good husband, and of Gawain, the light lover, in
that very Thuringia where a generation later the lap
of St. Elizabeth was full with roses. A Connaught
Bishop told his people a while since that they 'should
never read stories about the degrading passion of
love,' and one can only suppose that being ignorant
of a chief glory of his Church, he has never under-
stood that this new puritanism is but an English
cuckoo.

AN IRISH NATIONAL THEATRE.

[The performance of Mr. Synge's *Shadow of the Glen*
started a quarrel with the extreme national party, and the
following paragraphs are from letters written in the play's
defence. The organ of the party was at the time *The United
Irishman* (now *Sinn Fein*), but the first severe attack began in
The Independent. *The United Irishman*, however, took up
the quarrel, and from that on has attacked almost every play
produced at our theatre, and the suspicion it managed to arouse
among the political clubs against Mr. Synge especially led
a few years later to the organised attempt to drive *The Playboy
of the Western World* from the stage.]

When we were all fighting about the selection of
books for the New Irish Library some ten years ago, we
had to discuss the question, What is National Poetry?
In those days a patriotic young man would have
thought but poorly of himself if he did not believe
that *The Spirit of the Nation* was great lyric poetry,
and a much finer kind of poetry than Shelley's *Ode
to the West Wind*, or Keats's *Ode to a Grecian Urn*.
When two or three of us denied this, we were told
that we had effeminate tastes or that we were putting
Ireland in a bad light before her enemies. If one
said that *The Spirit of the Nation* was but salutary
rhetoric, England might overhear us and take up the
cry. We said it, and who will say that Irish litera-
ture has not a greater name in the world to-day than
it had ten years ago?

To-day there is another question that we must
make up our minds about, and an even more press-
ing one, What is a National Theatre? A man may
write a book of lyrics if he have but a friend or two
that will care for them, but he cannot write a good
play if there are not audiences to listen to it. If we

think that a national play must be as near as possible a page out of *The Spirit of the Nation* put into dramatic form, and mean to go on thinking it to the end, then we may be sure that this generation will not see the rise in Ireland of a theatre that will reflect the life of Ireland as the Scandinavian theatre reflects the Scandinavian life. The brazen head has an unexpected way of falling to pieces. We have a company of admirable and disinterested players, and the next few months will, in all likelihood, decide whether a great work for this country is to be accomplished. The poetry of Young Ireland, when it was an attempt to change or strengthen opinion, was rhetoric; but it became poetry when patriotism was transformed into a personal emotion by the events of life, as in that lamentation written by Doheny on his keeping among the hills. Literature is always personal, always one man's vision of the world, one man's experience, and it can only be popular when men are ready to welcome the visions of others. A community that is opinion-ridden, even when those opinions are in themselves noble, is likely to put its creative minds into some sort of a prison. If creative minds preoccupy themselves with incidents from the political history of Ireland, so much the better, but we must not enforce them to select those incidents. If in the sincere working-out of their plot, they alight on a moral that is obviously and directly serviceable to the National cause, so much the better, but we must not force that moral upon them. I am a Nationalist, and certain of my intimate friends have made Irish politics the business of their lives, and this made certain thoughts habitual with me, and an accident made these thoughts take fire in such a way that I could give them dramatic expression. I had a very vivid dream one night, and I made *Cathleen ni Houlihan* out of this dream. But if some external necessity had forced me to write nothing but drama with an obviously patriotic intention, instead of letting my work shape itself under the casual impulses of dreams and daily thoughts, I would have lost, in a short time, the power to write movingly upon any theme. I could have aroused opinion; but I could not have touched the heart, for I would have been busy at the oakum-picking that is not the less mere journalism for being in dramatic form. Above all, we must not say that certain incidents which have been a part of literature in all other lands are forbidden to us. It may be our duty, as it has been the duty of many dramatic movements, to bring new kinds of subjects into the theatre, but it cannot be our duty to make the bounds of drama narrower. For instance, we are told that the English theatre is immoral, because it is pre-occupied with the husband, the wife and the lover. It is, perhaps, too exclusively pre-occupied with that subject, and it is certain it has not shed any new light upon it for a considerable time, but a subject that inspired Homer and about half the great literature of the world will, one doubts not, be a necessity to our National Theatre also. Literature is, to my mind, the great teaching power of the world, the ultimate creator of all values, and it is this, not only in the sacred books whose power everybody acknowledges, but by every movement of imagination in song or story or drama that height of intensity and sincerity has made literature at all. Literature must take the responsibility of its power, and keep all its freedom: it must be like the spirit and like the wind that blows where it listeth, it must claim its right to pierce through every crevice of human nature, and to describe the relation of the soul and the heart to the facts of life and of law, and to describe that relation as it is, not as we would have it be, and in so far as it fails to do this it fails to give us that foundation of understanding and charity for whose lack our moral sense can be but cruelty. It must be as incapable of telling a lie as nature, and it must sometimes say before all the virtues, 'The greatest of these is charity.' Sometimes the patriot will have to falter and the wife to desert her home, and neither be followed by divine vengeance or man's judgment. At other moments it must be content to judge without remorse, compelled by nothing but its own capricious spirit that has yet its message from the foundation of the world. Aristophanes held up the people of Athens to ridicule, and even prouder of that spirit than of themselves, they invited the foreign ambassadors to the spectacle.

I would sooner our theatre failed through the indifference or hostility of our audiences than gained an immense popularity by any loss of freedom. I ask nothing that my masters have not asked for, but I ask all that they were given. I ask no help that would limit our freedom from either official or patriotic hands, though I am glad of the help of any who love the arts so dearly that they would not bring them into even honourable captivity. A good Nationalist is, I suppose, one who is ready to give up a great deal that he may preserve to his country whatever part of her possessions he is best fitted to guard, and that theatre where the capricious spirit that bloweth as it listeth has for a moment found a dwelling-place, has good right to call itself a National Theatre.

THE THEATRE, THE PULPIT, AND THE NEWSPAPERS.

I was very well content when I read an unmeasured attack in *The Independent* on the Irish National Theatre. There had, as yet, been no performance, but the attack was confident, and it was evident that the writer's ears were full of rumours and whisperings. One knew that some such attack was inevitable, for every dramatic movement that brought any new power into literature arose among precisely these misunderstandings and animosities. Drama, the most immediately powerful form of literature, the most vivid image of life, finds itself opposed, as no other form of literature does, to those enemies of life, the chimeras of the Pulpit and the Press. When a country has not begun to care for literature, or has forgotten the taste for it, and most modern countries seem to pass through this stage, these chimeras are hatched in every basket. Certain generalisations are everywhere substituted for life. Instead of individual men and women and living virtues differing as one star differeth from another in glory, the public imagination is full of personified averages, partisan fictions, rules of life that would drill everybody into the one posture, habits that are like the pinafores of charity-school children. The priest, trained to keep his mind on the strength of his Church and the weakness of his congregation, would have all mankind painted with a halo or with horns. Literature is nothing to him, he has to remember that Seaghan the Fool might take to drinking again if he knew of pleasant Falstaff, and that Paudeen might run after Red Sarah again if some strange chance put Plutarch's tale of Anthony or Shakespeare's play into his hands, and he is in a hurry to shut out of the schools that Pandora's box, *The Golden Treasury.* The newspaper he reads of a morning has not only the haloes and horns of the vestry, but it has crowns and fools' caps of its own. Life, which in its essence is always surprising, always taking some new shape, always individualising, is nothing to it, it has to move men in squads, to keep them in uniform, with their faces to the right enemy, and enough hate in their hearts to make the muskets go off. It may know its business well, but its business is building and ours is shattering. We cannot linger very long in this great dim temple where the wooden images sit all round upon thrones, and where the worshippers kneel, not knowing whether they tremble because their gods are dead or because they fear they may be alive. In the idol-house every god, every demon, every virtue, every vice, has been given its permanent form, its hundred hands, its elephant trunk, its monkey head. The man of letters looks at those kneeling worshippers who have given up life for a posture, whose nerves have dried up in the contemplation of lifeless wood. He swings his silver hammer and the keepers of the temple cry out, prophesying evil, but he must not mind their cries and their prophecies, but break the wooden necks in two and throw down the wooden bodies. Life will put living bodies in their place till new image-brokers have set up their benches.

Whenever literature becomes powerful, the priest,

whose forerunner imagined St. Patrick driving his chariot-wheels over his own erring sister, has to acknowledge, or to see others acknowledge, that there is no evil that men and women may not be driven into by their virtues all but as readily as by their vices, and the politician, that it is not always clean hands that serve a country or foul hands that ruin it. He may even have to say at last, as an old man who had spent many years in prison to serve a good cause said to me, 'There never was a cause so evil that it has not been served by good men for what seemed to them sufficient reasons.' And if the priest or the politician should say to the man of letters, 'Into how dangerous a state of mind are you not bringing us?' the man of letters can but answer, 'It is dangerous, indeed,' and say, like my Seanchan, 'When did we promise safety?'

Thought takes the same form age after age, and the things that people have said to me about this intellectual movement of ours have, I doubt not, been said in every country to every writer who was a disturber of the old life. When *The Countess Cathleen* was produced, the very girls in the shops complained to us that to describe an Irishwoman as selling her soul to the devil was to slander the country. The silver hammer had threatened, as it seems, one of those personifications of an average. Someone said to me a couple of weeks ago, 'If you put on the stage any play about marriage that does not point its moral clearly, you will make it difficult for us to go on attacking the English theatre for its immorality.' Again, we were disordering the squads, the muskets might not all point in the same direction.

Now that these opinions have found a leader and a voice in *The Independent*, it is easy at anyrate to explain how much one differs from them. I had spoken of the capricious power of the artist and compared it to the capricious movements of a wild creature, and *The Independent*, speaking quite logically from its point of view, tells me that these movements were only interesting when 'under restraint.' The writers of the Anglo-Irish movement, it says, 'will never consent to serve except on terms that never could or should be conceded.' I had spoken of the production of foreign masterpieces, but it considers that foreign masterpieces would be very dangerous. I had asked in *Samhain* for audiences sufficiently tolerant to enable the half-dozen minds who are likely to be the dramatic imagination of Ireland for this generation to put their own thought and their own characters into their work. That is to say, I had asked for the amount of freedom which every nation has given to its dramatic writers. But the newspaper hopes and believes that no 'such tolerance will be extended to Mr. Yeats and his friends.'

I have written these lines to explain our thoughts and intentions to many personal friends, who live too deep in the labour of politics to give the thought to these things that we have given, and because not only in our theatre, but in all matters of national life, we have need of a new discovery of life—of more precise thought, of a more perfect sincerity. I would see, in every branch of our National propaganda, young men who would have the sincerity and the precision of those Russian revolutionists that Kropotkin and Stepniak tell us of, men who would never use an argument to convince others which would not convince themselves, who would not make a mob drunk with a passion they could not share, and who would above all seek for fine things for their own sake, and for precise knowledge for its own sake, and not for its momentary use. One can serve one's country alone out of the abundance of one's own heart, and it is labour enough to be certain one is in the right, without having to be certain that one's thought is expedient also.

1904

THE DRAMATIC MOVEMENT

THE National Theatre Society has had great difficulties because of the lack of any suitable playhouse. It has been forced to perform in halls without proper lighting for the stage, and almost without dressing-rooms, and with level floors in the auditorium that prevented all but the people in the front row from seeing properly. These halls are expensive too, and the players of poetical drama in an age of musical comedy have light pockets. But now a generous English friend, Miss Horniman, has re-arranged and in part re-built, at very considerable expense, the old Mechanic's Institute Theatre, now the Abbey Theatre, and given us the use of it without any charge, and I need not say that she has gained our gratitude, as she will gain the gratitude of our audience. The work of decoration and alteration has been done by Irishmen, and everything, with the exception of some few things that are not made here, or not of a good enough quality, has been manufactured in Ireland. The stained glass in the entrance hall is the work of Miss Sarah Purser and her apprentices, the large copper mirror frames are from the new metal works at Youghal, and the pictures of some of our players are by an Irish artist. These details and some details of form and colour in the building, as a whole, have been arranged by Miss Horniman herself.

K

Having been given the free use of this Theatre, we may look upon ourselves as the first endowed Theatre in any English-speaking country, the English-speaking countries and Venezuela being the only countries which have never endowed their theatres; but the correspondents who write for parts in our plays or posts in the Theatre at a salary are in error. We are, and must be for some time to come, contented to find our work its own reward, the player giving* his work, and the playwright his, for nothing; and though this cannot go on always, we start our winter very cheerfully with a capital of some forty pounds. We playwrights can only thank these players, who have given us the delight of seeing our work so well performed, working with so much enthusiasm, with so much patience, that they have found for themselves a lasting place among the artists, the only aristocracy that has never been sold in the market or seen the people rise up against it.

It is a necessary part of our plan to find out how to perform plays for little money, for it is certain that every increase in expenditure has lowered the quality of dramatic art itself, by robbing the dramatist of freedom in experiment, and by withdrawing attention from his words and from the work of the players. Sometimes one friend or another has helped us with costumes or scenery, but the expense has never been very great, ten or twenty pounds being enough in most cases for quite a long play. These friends have all accepted the principles I have explained from

* The players, though not the playwrights, are now all paid.—W.B.Y., *March*, 1908.

time to time in *Samhain*, but they have interpreted them in various ways according to their temperament.

Miss Horniman staged *The King's Threshold* at her own expense, and she both designed and made the costumes. The costumes for the coming performances of *On Baile's Strand* are also her work and her gift and her design. She made and paid for the costumes in *The Shadowy Waters*, but in this case followed a colour-scheme of mine. The colour-scheme in *The Hour-Glass*, our first experiment, was worked out by Mr. Robert Gregory and myself, and the costumes were made by Miss Lavelle, a member of the company; while Mr. Robert Gregory has designed the costumes and scenery for *Kincora*. As we gradually accumulate costumes in all the main colours and shades, we will be able to get new effects by combining them in different ways without buying new ones. Small dramatic societies, and our example is beginning to create a number, not having so many friends as we have, might adopt a simpler plan, suggested to us by a very famous decorative artist. Let them have one suit of clothes for a king, another for a queen, another for a fighting-man, another for a messenger, and so on, and if these clothes are loose enough to fit different people, they can perform any romantic play that comes without new cost. The audience would soon get used to this way of symbolising, as it were, the different ranks and classes of men, and as the king would wear, no matter what the play might be, the same crown and robe, they could have them very fine in the end. Now, one wealthy theatre-goer and now another might add a pearl to the queen's necklace, or a jewel to her crown, and be the more regular in attendance at the theatre because that gift shone out there like a good deed.

We can hardly do all we hope unless there are many more of these little societies to be centres of dramatic art and of the allied arts. But a very few actors went from town to town in ancient Greece, finding everywhere more or less well trained singers among the principal townsmen to sing the chorus that had otherwise been the chief expense. In the days of the stock companies two or three well-known actors would go from town to town finding actors for all the minor parts in the local companies. If we are to push our work into the small towns and villages, local dramatic clubs must take the place of the old stock companies. A good-sized town should be able to give us a large enough audience for our whole, or nearly our whole, company to go there; but the need for us is greater in those small towns where the poorest kind of farce and melodrama have gone and Shakespearean drama has not gone, and it is here that we will find it hardest to get intelligent audiences. If a dramatic club existed in one of the larger towns near, they could supply us not only with actors, should we need them, in their own town, but with actors when we went to the small towns and to the villages where the novelty of any kind of drama would make success certain. These clubs would play in Gaelic far better than we can hope to, for they would have native Gaelic speakers, and should we succeed in stirring the imagination of the people enough to keep the rivalry between plays in English and Irish to a rivalry in quality, the certain development of two schools with distinct though very kindred ideals would increase the energy and compass of our art.

At a time when drama was more vital than at present, unpaid actors, and actors with very little training, have influenced it deeply. The Mystery Plays and the Miracle Plays got their players at no great distance from the Church door, and the classic drama of France had for a forerunner performances of Greek and Latin Classics, given by students and people of quality, and even at its height Racine wrote two of his most famous tragedies to be played by young girls at school. This was before acting had got so far away from our natural instincts of expression. When the play is in verse, or in rhythmical prose, it does not gain by the change, and a company of amateurs, if they love literature, and are not self-conscious, and really do desire to do well, can often make a better hand of it than the ordinary professional company.

The greater number of their plays will, in all likelihood, be comedies of Irish country life, and here they need not fear competition, for they will know an Irish countryman as no professional can know him; but whatever they play, they will have one advantage the English amateur has not: there is in their blood a natural capacity for acting, and they have never, like him, become the mimics of well-known actors. The arts have always lost something of their sap when they have been cut off from the people as a whole; and when the theatre is perfectly alive, the audience, as at the Gaelic drama to-day in Gaelic-

speaking districts, feels itself to be almost a part of
the play. I have never felt that the dignity of art
was imperilled when the audience at Dr. Hyde's *An
Posadh* cheered the bag of flour or the ham lent by
some local shopkeepers to increase the bridal gifts.
It was not merely because of its position in the play
that the Greek chorus represented the people, and
the old ballad singers waited at the end of every verse
till their audience had taken up the chorus; while
Ritual, the most powerful form of drama, differs from
the ordinary form, because everyone who hears it is
also a player. Our modern theatre, with the seats
always growing more expensive, and its dramatic art
drifting always from the living impulse of life, and
becoming more and more what Rossetti would have
called 'soulless self-reflections of man's skill,' no
longer gives pleasure to any imaginative mind. It is
easy for us to hate England in this country, and we
give that hatred something of nobility if we turn it
now and again into hatred of the vulgarity of com-
mercial syndicates, of all that commercial finish and
pseudo-art she has done so much to cherish. Mr.
Standish O'Grady has quoted somebody as saying
'the passions must be held in reverence, they must
not, they cannot be excited at will,' and the noble
using of that old hatred will win for us sympathy and
attention from all artists and people of good taste,
and from those of England more than anywhere, for
there is the need greatest.

Before this part of our work can be begun, it will be
necessary to create a household of living art in Dublin,
with principles that have become habits, and a public

that has learnt to care for a play because it is a play, and not because it is serviceable to some cause. Our patent is not so wide as we had hoped for, for we had hoped to have a patent as little restricted as that of the Gaiety or the Theatre Royal. We were, however, vigorously opposed by these theatres and by the Queen's Theatre, and the Solicitor-General, to meet them half way, has restricted our patent to plays written by Irishmen or on Irish subjects or to foreign masterpieces, provided these masterpieces are not English. This has been done to make our competition against the existing theatres as unimportant as possible. It does not directly interfere with the work of our society to any serious extent, but it would have indirectly helped our work had such bodies as the Elizabethan Stage Society, which brought *Everyman* to Dublin some years ago, been able to hire the theatre from Miss Horniman, when it is not wanted by us, and to perform there without the limitations imposed by a special license.

Everything that creates a theatrical audience is an advantage to us, and the small number of seats in our theatre would have kept away that kind of drama, in whatever language, which spoils an audience for good work.

The enquiry itself was not a little surprising, for the legal representatives of the theatres, being the representatives of Musical Comedy, were very anxious for the morals of the town. I had spoken of the Independent Theatre, and a lawyer wanted to know if a play of mine which attacked the institution of marriage had not been performed by it recently. I had spoken of M. Maeterlinck and of his indebtedness to a theatre somewhat similar to our own, and one of our witnesses, who knew no more about it than the questioner, was asked if a play by M. Maeterlinck called *L'Intruse* had not been so immoral that it was received with a cry of horror in London. I have written no play about marriage, and the Independent Theatre died some twelve years ago, and *L'Intruse* might be played in a nursery with no worse effects than a little depression of spirits. Our opponents having thus protested against our morals, went home with the fees of Musical Comedy in their pockets.

For all this, we are better off so far as the law is concerned than we would be in England. The theatrical law of Ireland was made by the Irish Parliament, and though the patent system, the usual method of the time, has outlived its use and come to an end everywhere but in Ireland, we must be grateful to that ruling caste of free spirits, that being free themselves they left the theatre in freedom. In England there is a censor, who forbids you to take a subject from the Bible, or from politics, or to picture public characters, or certain moral situations which are the foundation of some of the greatest plays of the world. When I was at the great American Catholic University of Notre-Dame I heard that the students had given a performance of *Œdipus the King*, and *Œdipus the King* is forbidden in London. A censorship created in the eighteenth century by Walpole, because somebody had written against election bribery, has been distorted by a puritanism, which is not the less an English invention for being a pretended hatred of vice and a

real hatred of intellect. Nothing has ever suffered
so many persecutions as the intellect, though it is
never persecuted under its own name. It is but ac-
cording to old usage when a law that cherishes Musical
Comedy and permits to every second melodrama the
central situation of *The Sign of the Cross*, attempted
rape, becomes one of the secondary causes of the
separation of the English Theatre from life. It does
not interfere with anything that makes money, and
Musical Comedy, with its hints and innuendoes, and
its consistently low view of life, makes a great deal,
for money is always respectable ; but would a group
of artists and students see once again the master-
pieces of the world, they would have to hide from the
law as if they had been a school of thieves ; or were
we to take with us to London that beautiful Nativity
Play of Dr. Hyde's, which was performed in Sligo
Convent a few months ago, that holy vision of the
central story of the world, as it is seen through the
minds and the traditions of the poor, the constables
might upset the cradle. And yet it is precisely these
stories of The Bible that have all to themselves, in
the imagination of English people, especially of the
English poor, the place they share in this country
with the stories of Fion and of Oisin and of Patrick.

Milton set the story of Sampson into the form of
a Greek play, because he knew that Sampson was,
in the English imagination, what Herakles was in the
imagination of Greece ; and I have never been able to
see any other subjects for an English Dramatist who
looked for some common ground between his own
mind and simpler minds. An English poet of genius
once told me that he would have tried his hand in

plays for the people, if they knew any story the censor would pass, except Jack and the Beanstalk.

The Gaelic League has its great dramatic opportunity because of the abundance of stories known in Irish-speaking districts, and because of the freedom of choice and of treatment the leaders of a popular movement can have if they have a mind for it. The Gaelic plays acted and published during the year selected their subjects from the popular mind, but the treatment is disappointing. Dr. Hyde, dragged from gathering to gathering by the necessities of the movement, has written no new play; and Father Peter O'Leary has thrown his dramatic power, which is remarkable, into an imaginative novel. Father Dineen has published a little play that has some life-like dialogue, but the action is sometimes irrelevant, and the motives of the principal character are vague and confused, as if it were written in a hurry. Father Dineen seems to know that he has not done his best, for he describes it as an attempt to provide more vivid dialogue for beginners than is to be found in the reading-books rather than a drama. An anonymous writer has written a play called *The Money of the Narrow Cross*, which tells a very simple tale, like that of a child's book, simply and adequately. It is very slight, in low relief as it were, but if its writer is a young man it has considerable promise.

A Play called *Seaghan na Scuab* was described in the *United Irishman* as the best play ever written in Irish; but though the subject of it is a dramatic old folk-tale, which has shown its vigour by rooting

itself in many countries, the treatment is confused
and conventional and there is a flatness of dialogue
unusual in these plays.   There is, however, an occa-
sional sense of comic situation which may come to
something if its writer will work seriously at his craft.
One is afraid of quenching the smoking flax, but this
play was selected for performance at the *Oireachtas*
before a vast audience in the Rotunda.   It was accom-
panied by *The Doctor* in English and Irish, written by
Mr. O'Beirne, and performed by the Tawin players,
who brought it from their seaside village in Galway.
Mr. O'Beirne deserves the greatest praise for getting
this company together, as well as for all he has done
to give the Tawin people a new pleasure in their
language ; but I think a day will come when he will
not be grateful to the *Oireachtas* Committee for bring-
ing this first crude work of his into the midst of so
many thousand people.   It would be very hard for a
much more experienced dramatist to make anything
out of the ugly violence, the threadbare, second-hand
imaginations that flow in upon one out of the
newspapers, when one has founded one's work on
proselytizing zeal, instead of one's experience of life
and one's curiosity about it.   These two were the
only plays, out of a number that have been played in
Irish, that I have seen this year.   I went to Galway
Feis, like many others, to see Dr. Hyde's *Lost Saint*,
for I had missed every performance of it hitherto
though I had read it to many audiences in America,
and I awaited the evening with some little excitement.
Although the *Lost Saint* was on the programme, an
Anti-Emigration play was put in its place.   I did not
wait for this, but, whatever its merits, it is not likely

to have contained anything so beautiful as the old man's prayer in the other: 'O Lord, O God, take pity on this little soft child. Put wisdom in his head, cleanse his heart, scatter the mist from his mind and let him learn his lessons like the other boys. O Lord, Thou wert Thyself young one time; take pity on youth. O Lord, Thou, Thyself, shed tears; dry the tears of this little lad. Listen, O Lord, to the prayer of Thy servant, and do not keep from him this little thing he is asking of Thee. O Lord, bitter are the tears of a child, sweeten them: deep are the thoughts of a child, quiet them: sharp is the grief of a child, take it from him: soft is the heart of a child, do not harden it.'

A certain number of propagandist plays are unavoidable in a popular movement like the Gaelic revival, but they may drive out everything else. The plays, while Father Peter O'Leary and Father Dineen and Dr. Hyde were the most popular writers and the chief influence, were full of the traditional folk-feeling that is the mastering influence in all old Irish literature. Father O'Leary chose for his subjects a traditional story of a trick played upon a simple villager, a sheep-stealer frightened by what seemed to him a ghost, the quarrels between Maeve and Aleel of Cruachan; Father Dineen chose for his a religious crisis, alive as with the very soul of tragedy, or a well sacred to the fairies; while Dr. Hyde celebrated old story-tellers and poets, and old saints, and the Mother of God with the countenance she wears in Irish eyes. Hundreds of men scattered through the world, angry at the spectacle of modern vulgarity, rejoiced in this movement, for it seemed impossible for anything begun in so high a spirit, so inspired by whatever is ancient, or simple, or noble, to sink into the common base level of our thought. This year one has heard little of the fine work, and a great deal about plays that get an easy cheer, because they make no discoveries in human nature, but repeat the opinions of the audience, or the satire of its favourite newspapers. I am only speaking of the plays of a year, and that is but a short period in what one hopes may be a great movement, but it is not wise to say, as do many Gaelic Leaguers, who know the weaknesses of their movement, that if the present thinks but of grammar and propaganda the future will do all the rest. A movement will often in its first fire of enthusiasm create more works of genius than whole easy-going centuries that come after it.

Nearly everything that is greatest as English prose was written in a generation or two after the first beautiful use of prose in England : and Mistral has made the poems of modern Provençe, as well as reviving and all but inventing the language : for genius is more often of the spring than of the middle green of the year. We cannot settle times and seasons, flowering-time and harvest-time are not in our hands, but we are to blame if genius comes and we do not gather in the fruit or the blossom. Very often we can do no more for the man of genius than to distract him as little as may be with the common business of the day. His own work is more laborious than any other, for not only is thought harder than action, as Goethe said, but he must brood over his work so long and so unbrokenly that he find there all his patriotism, all his passion, his religion even—it is not only those that sweep a floor that are obedient to heaven—until at last he can cry with Paracelsus, 'In this crust of bread I have found all the stars and all the heavens.'

The following new plays were produced by the National Theatre Society during the last twelve months :—*The Shadow of the Glen* and *Riders to the Sea*, by Mr. J. M. Synge ; *Broken Soil*, by Mr. Colm ; *The Townland of Tamney*, by Mr. Seumas MacManus; *The Shadowy Waters* and *The King's Threshold*, by myself. The following plays were revived :—*Deirdre*, by A.E. ; *Twenty-five*, by Lady Gregory ; *Cathleen ni Houlihan*, *The Pot of Broth*, and *The Hour-Glass*, by myself. We could have given more plays, but difficulties about the place of performance, the shifting of scenery from where we rehearsed to where we acted, and so on, always brought a great deal of labour upon the Society. The Society went to London in March and gave two performances at The Royalty to full houses. They played there Mr. Synge's two plays, Mr. Colm's play, and my *King's Threshold* and *Pot of Broth*. We were commended by the critics with generous sympathy, and had an enthusiastic and distinguished audience.

We have many plays awaiting performance during the coming winter. Mr. Synge has written us a play in three acts called *The Well of the Saints*, full, as few works of our time are, with temperament, and of a true and yet bizarre beauty. Lady Gregory has written us an historical tragedy in three acts about King Brian and a very merry comedy of country life. Mr. Bernard Shaw has written us a play* in four acts, his first experiment in Irish satire; Mr. Tarpey, an Irishman whose comedy *Windmills* was successfully prepared by the Stage Society some years ago, a little play which I have not yet seen; and Mr. Boyle, a village comedy in three acts; and I hear of other plays by competent hands that are coming to us. My own *Baile's Strand* is in rehearsal, and I hope to have ready for the spring a play on the subject of *Deirdre*, with choruses somewhat in the Greek manner. We are, of course, offered from all parts of the world great quantities of plays which are impossible for literary or dramatic reasons. Some of them have a look of having been written for the commercial theatre and of having been sent to us on rejection. It will save trouble if I point out that a play which seems to its writer to promise an ordinary London or New York success is very unlikely to please us, or succeed with our audience if it did. Writers who have a better ambition should get some mastery of their art in little plays before spending many months of what is almost sure to be wasted labour on several acts.

We were invited to play in the St. Louis Exhibition, but thought that our work should be in Ireland for the present, and had other reasons for refusing.

A Company, which has been formed in America by Miss Witcherly, who played in *Everyman* during a part of its tour in America, to take some of our plays on tour, has begun with three one-act plays of mine, *Cathleen ni Houlihan*, *The Hour-Glass*, and *The Land*

* *John Bull's Other Island.*

of Heart's Desire.   It announces on its circulars that it is following the methods of our Theatre.

Though the commercial theatre of America is as unashamedly commercial as the English, there is a far larger audience interested in fine drama than here. When I was lecturing in, I think, Philadelphia—one town mixes with another in my memory at times— some one told me that he had seen the *Duchess of Malfi* played there by one of the old stock companies in his boyhood; and *Everyman* has been far more of a success in America than anywhere else. They have numberless University towns each with its own character and with an academic life animated by a zeal and by an imagination unknown in these countries.   There is nearly everywhere that leaven of highly-cultivated men and women so much more necessary to a good theatrical audience to-day than were ever Raleigh and Sidney, when the groundling could remember the folk-songs and the imaginative folk-life.   The more an age is busy with temporary things, the more must it look for leadership in matters of art to men and women whose business or whose leisure has made the great writers of the world their habitual company. Literature is not journalism because it can turn the imagination to whatever is essential and unchanging in life.

FIRST PRINCIPLES.

Two Irish writers had a controversy a month ago, and they accused one another of being unable to think, with entire sincerity, though it was obvious to uncommitted minds that neither had any lack of vigorous thought. But they had a different meaning when they spoke of thought, for the one, though in actual life he is the most practical man I know, meant thought as Paschal, as Montaigne, as Shakespeare, or as, let us say, Emerson, understood it—a reverie about the adventures of the soul, or of the personality, or some obstinate questioning of the riddle. Many who have to work hard always make time for this reverie, but it comes more easily to the leisured, and in this it is like a broken heart, which is, a Dublin newspaper assured us lately, impossible to a busy man. The other writer had in mind, when he spoke of thought, the shaping energy that keeps us busy, and the obstinate questionings he had most respect for were, how to change the method of government, how to change the language, how to revive our manufactures, and whether it is the Protestant or the Catholic that scowls at the other with the darker scowl. Ireland is so poor, so misgoverned, that a great portion of the imagination of the land must give itself to a very passionate consideration of questions like these, and yet it is precisely these loud questions that drive away the reveries that incline the imagination to the lasting work of literature and give, together with religion, sweetness,

and nobility, and dignity to life. We should desire
no more from these propagandist thinkers than that
they carry out their work, as far as possible, without
making it more difficult for those, fitted by Nature
or by circumstance for another kind of thought, to
do their work also; and certainly it is not well that
Martha chide at Mary, for they have the One Master
over them.

When one all but despairs, as one does at times,
of Ireland welcoming a National Literature in this
generation, it is because we do not leave ourselves
enough of time, or of quiet, to be interested in men
and women. A writer in *The Leader*, who is unknown
to me, elaborates this argument in an article full of
beauty and dignity. He is speaking of our injustice
to one another, and he says that we are driven into
injustice 'not wantonly but inevitably, and at call
of the exacting qualities of the great things. Until
this latter dawning, the genius of Ireland has been
too preoccupied really to concern itself about men
and women; in its drama they play a subordinate
part, born tragic comedians though all the sons and
daughters of the land are. A nation is the heroic
theme we follow, a mourning, wasted land its moving
spirit; the impersonal assumes personality for us.'
When I wrote my *Countess Cathleen*, I thought, of
course, chiefly of the actual picture that was forming
before me, but there was a secondary meaning that
came into my mind continuously. 'It is the soul of
one that loves Ireland,' I thought, 'plunging into
unrest, seeming to lose itself, to bargain itself away
to the very wickedness of the world, and to surrender

what is eternal for what is temporary,' and I know
that this meaning seemed natural to others, for that
great orator, J. F. Taylor, who was not likely to
have searched very deeply into any work of mine,
for he cared little for mine, or, indeed, any modern
work, turned the play into such a parable in one of
his speeches.

There is no use being angry with necessary con-
ditions, or failing to see that a man who is busy with
some reform that can only be carried out in a flame
of energetic feeling, will not only be indifferent to
what seems to us the finer kind of thinking, but that
he will support himself by generalisations that seem
untrue to the man of letters. A little play, *The
Rising of the Moon*, which is in the present number
of *Samhain*, and is among those we are to produce
during the winter, has, for instance, roused the sus-
picions of a very resolute leader of the people, who
has a keen eye for rats behind the arras. A Fenian
ballad-singer partly converts a policeman, and is it
not unwise under any circumstances to show a police-
man in so favourable a light? It is well known that
many of the younger policemen were Fenians: but
it is necessary that the Dublin crowds should be kept
of so high a heart that they will fight the police at
any moment. Are not morals greater than literature?
Others have objected to Mr. Synge's *Shadow of the
Glen* because Irish women, being more chaste than
those of England and Scotland, are a valuable part
of our national argument. Mr. Synge should not,
it is said by some, have chosen an exception for the
subject of his play, for who knows but the English

may misunderstand him? Some even deny that such
a thing could happen at all, while others that know
the country better, or remember the statistics, say
that it could but should never have been staged. All
these arguments, by their methods even more than
by what they have tried to prove, misunderstand how
literature does its work. Men of letters have some-
times said that the characters of a romance or of a
play must be typical. They mean that the character
must be typical of something which exists in all men
because the writer has found it in his own mind. It
is one of the most inexplicable things about human
nature that a writer, with a strange temperament, an
Edgar Allan Poe, let us say, made what he is by
conditions that never existed before, can create per-
sonages and lyric emotions, which startle us by being
at once bizarre and an image of our own secret
thoughts. Are we not face to face with the micro-
cosm, mirroring everything in universal nature? It
is no more necessary for the characters created by a
romance writer, or a dramatist, to have existed before,
than for his own personality to have done so; char-
acters and personality alike, as is perhaps true in the
instance of Poe, may draw half their life not from
the solid earth but from some dreamy drug. This is
true even of historical drama, for it was Goethe, the
founder of the historical drama of Germany, who
said 'we do the people of history the honour of
naming after them the creations of our own minds.'
All that a dramatic writer need do is to persuade us,
during the two hours' traffic of the stage, that the
events of his play did really happen. He must
know enough of the life of his country, or of history,

to create this illusion, but no matter how much he knows, he will fail if his audience is not ready to give up something of the dead letter. If his mind is full of energy he will not be satisfied with little knowledge, but he will be far more likely to alter incidents and characters, wilfully even as it may seem, than to become a literal historian. It was one of the complaints against Shakespeare, in his own day, that he made Sir John Falstaff out of a praiseworthy old Lollard preacher. One day, as he sat over Holinshed's History of England, he persuaded himself that Richard the Second, with his French culture, 'his too great friendliness to his friends,' his beauty of mind, and his fall before dry, repelling Bolingbroke, would be a good image for an accustomed mood of fanciful, impracticable lyricism in his own mind. The historical Richard has passed away for ever and the Richard of the play lives more intensely, it seems, than did ever living man. Yet Richard the Second, as Shakespeare made him, could never have been born before the Renaissance, before the Italian influence, or even one hour before the innumerable streams that flowed in upon Shakespeare's mind; the innumerable experiences we can never know, brought Shakespeare to the making of him. He is typical not because he ever existed, but because he has made us know of something in our own minds we had never known of had he never been imagined.

Our propagandists have twisted this theory of the men of letters into its direct contrary, and when they say that a writer should make typical characters they mean personifications of averages, of statistics,

or even personified opinions, or men and women so
faintly imagined that there is nothing about them to
separate them from the crowd, as it appears to our
hasty eyes.   We must feel that we could engage a
hundred others to wear the same livery as easily as
we could engage a coachman. We must never forget
that we are engaging them to be the ideal young
peasant, or the true patriot, or the happy Irish wife,
or the policeman of our prejudices, or to express
some other of those invaluable generalisations, with-
out which our practical movements would lose their
energy.   Who is there that likes a coachman to be
too full of human nature, when he has his livery on ?
No one man is like another, but one coachman should
be as like another as possible, though he may assert
himself a little when he meets the gardener.   The
patriots would impose on us heroes and heroines,
like those young couples in the Gaelic plays, who
might all change brides or bridegrooms in the dance
and never find out the difference. The personifica-
tions need not be true even, if they are about our
enemy, for it might be more difficult to fight out our
necessary fight if we remembered his virtue at wrong
moments ; and might not Teig and Bacach, that are
light in the head, go over to his party?

   Ireland is indeed poor, is indeed hunted by mis-
fortune, and has indeed to give up much that makes
life desirable and lovely, but is she so very poor that
she can afford no better literature than this ? Perhaps
so, but if it is a Spirit from beyond the world that
decides when a nation shall awake into imaginative
energy, and no philosopher has ever found what
brings the moment, it cannot be for us to judge.

It may be coming upon us now, for it is certain that
we have more writers who are thinking, as men of
letters understand thought, than we have had for a
century, and he who wilfully makes their work
harder may be setting himself against the purpose
of that Spirit.

I would not be trying to form an Irish National
Theatre if I did not believe that there existed in
Ireland, whether in the minds of a few people or of
a great number I do not know, an energy of thought
about life itself, a vivid sensitiveness as to the reality
of things, powerful enough to overcome all those
phantoms of the night. One thing calls up its
contrary, unreality calls up reality, and, besides, life
here has been sufficiently perilous to make men
think. I do not think it a national prejudice that
makes me believe we are a harder, a more masterful
race than the comfortable English of our time, and
that this comes from an essential nearness to reality
of those few scattered people who have the right to
call themselves the Irish race. It is only in the
exceptions, in the few minds, where the flame has
burnt as it were pure, that one can see the permanent
character of a race. If one remembers the men who
have dominated Ireland for the last hundred and
fifty years, one understands that it is strength of
personality, the individualizing quality in a man,
that stirs Irish imagination most deeply in the end.
There is scarcely a man who has led the Irish people,
at any time, who may not give some day to a great
writer precisely that symbol he may require for the
expression of himself. The critical mind of Ireland

is far more subjugated than the critical mind of
England by the phantoms and misapprehensions of
politics and social necessity, but the life of Ireland
has rejected them more resolutely. Indeed, it is in
life itself in England that one finds the dominion of
what is not human life.

We have no longer in any country a literature as
great as the literature of the old world, and that is
because the newspapers, all kinds of second-rate
books, the preoccupation of men with all kinds of
practical changes, have driven the living imagination
out of the world. I have read hardly any books
this summer but Cervantes and Boccaccio and some
Greek plays. I have felt that these men, divided
from one another by so many hundreds of years,
had the same mind. It is we who are different ; and
then the thought would come to me, that has come
to me so often before, that they lived at times when
the imagination turned to life itself for excitement.
The world was not changing quickly about them.
There was nothing to draw their imagination from
the ripening of their fields, from the birth and death
of their children, from the destiny of their souls,
from all that is the unchanging substance of literature.
They had not to deal with the world in such great
masses that it could only be represented to their
minds by figures and by abstract generalisations.
Everything that their minds ran on came to them
vivid with the colour of the senses, and when they
wrote it was out of their own rich experience, and
they found their symbols of expression in things that
they had known all their life long. Their very

words were more vigorous than ours, for their phrases
came from a common mint, from the market, or the
tavern, or from the great poets of a still older time.
It is the change, that followed the Renaissance and
was completed by newspaper government and the
scientific movement, that has brought upon us all
these phrases and generalisations, made by minds
that would grasp what they have never seen.
Yesterday I went out to see the reddening apples
in the garden, and they faded from my imagination
sooner than they would have from the imagination
of that old poet, who made the songs of the seasons
for the Fianna, or out of Chaucer's, that celebrated
so many trees. Theories, opinions, these opinions
among the rest, flowed in upon me and blotted them
away. Even our greatest poets see the world with
preoccupied minds. Great as Shelley is, those theories
about the coming changes of the world, which he
has built up with so much elaborate passion, hurry
him from life continually. There is a phrase in
some old cabalistic writer about man falling into his
own circumference, and every generation we get
further away from life itself, and come more and
more under the influence which Blake had in his
mind when he said, 'Kings and Parliament seem to
me something other than human life.' We lose
our freedom more and more as we get away from
ourselves, and not merely because our minds are
overthrown by abstract phrases and generalisations,
reflections in a mirror that seem living, but because
we have turned the table of value upside down, and
believe that the root of reality is not in the centre but
somewhere in that whirling circumference. How can

we create like the ancients, while innumerable considerations of external probability or social utility or of what is becoming in so meritorious a person as ourselves, destroy the seeming irresponsible creative power that is life itself? Who to-day could set Richmond's and Richard's tents side by side on the battlefield, or make Don Quixote, mad as he was, mistake a windmill for a giant in broad daylight? And when I think of free-spoken Falstaff I know of no audience, but the tinkers of the roadside, that could encourage the artist to an equal comedy. The old writers were content if their inventions had but an emotional and moral consistency, and created out of themselves a fantastic, energetic, extravagant art. A Civilisation is very like a man or a woman, for it comes in but a few years into its beauty and its strength, and then, while many years go by, it gathers and makes order about it, the strength and beauty going out of it the while, until in the end it lies there with its limbs straightened out and a clean linen cloth folded upon it. That may well be, and yet we need not follow among the mourners, for it may be, before they are at the tomb, a messenger will run out of the hills and touch the pale lips with a red ember, and wake the limbs to the disorder and the tumult that is life. Though he does not come, even so we will keep from among the mourners and hold some cheerful conversation among ourselves; for has not Virgil, a knowledgeable man and a wizard, foretold that other Argonauts shall row between cliff and cliff, and other fair-haired Achæans sack another Troy?

Every argument carries us backwards to some religious conception, and in the end the creative energy of men depends upon their believing that they have, within themselves, something immortal and imperishable, and that all else is but as an image in a looking-glass. So long as that belief is not a formal thing, a man will create out of a joyful energy, seeking little for any external test of an impulse that may be sacred, and looking for no foundation outside life itself. If Ireland could escape from those phantoms of hers she might create, as did the old writers; for she has a faith that is as theirs, and keeps alive in the Gaelic traditions—and this has always seemed to me the chief intellectual value of Gaelic—a portion of the old imaginative life. When Dr. Hyde or Father Peter O'Leary is the writer, one's imagination goes straight to the century of Cervantes, and, having gone so far, one thinks at every moment that they will discover his energy. It is precisely because of this reason that one is indignant with those who would substitute for the ideas of the folk-life the rhetoric of the newspapers, who would muddy what had begun to seem a fountain of life with the feet of the mob. Is it impossible to revive Irish and yet to leave the finer intellects a sufficient mastery over the more gross, to prevent it from becoming, it may be, the language of a Nation, and yet losing all that has made it worthy of a revival, all that has made it a new energy in the mind?

Before the modern movement, and while it was but new, the ordinary man, whether he could read and write or not, was ready to welcome great literature.

When Ariosto found himself among the brigands, they repeated to him his own verses, and the audience in the Elizabethan Theatres must have been all but as clever as an Athenian audience. But to-day we come to understand great literature by a long preparation, or by some accident of nature, for we only begin to understand life when our minds have been purified of temporary interests by study.

But if literature has no external test, how are we to know that it is indeed literature? The only test that nature gives, to show when we obey her, is that she gives us happiness, and when we are no longer obedient she brings us to pain sooner or later. Is it not the same with the artist? The sign that she makes to him is that happiness we call delight in beauty. He can only convey this in its highest form after he has purified his mind with the great writers of the world; but their example can never be more than a preparation. If his art does not seem, when it comes, to be the creation of a new personality, in a few years it will not seem to be alive at all. If he is a dramatist his characters must have a like newness. If they could have existed before his days, or have been imagined before his day, we may be certain that the spirit of life is not in them in its fulness. This is because art, in its highest moments, is not a deliberate creation, but the creation of intense feeling, of pure life; and every feeling is the child of all past ages and would be different if even a moment had been left out. Indeed, is it not that delight in beauty, which tells the artist that he has imagined what may never die, itself but a delight in the permanent yet ever-changing

form of life, in her very limbs and lineaments? When
life has given it, has she given anything but herself?
Has she any other reward, even for the saints? If
one flies to the wilderness, is not that clear light that
falls about the soul when all irrelevant things have
been taken away, but life that has been about one
always, enjoyed in all its fulness at length? It is as
though she had put her arms about one, crying: 'My
beloved, you have given up everything for me.' If
a man spend all his days in good works till there is
no emotion in his heart that is not full of virtue, is
not the reward he prays for eternal life? The artist,
too, has prayers and a cloister, and if he do not turn
away from temporary things, from the zeal of the
reformer and the passion of revolution, that zealous
mistress will give him but a scornful glance.

What attracts one to drama is that it is, in the
most obvious way, what all the arts are upon a last
analysis. A farce and a tragedy are alike in this
that they are a moment of intense life. An action
is taken out of all other actions ; it is reduced to its
simple form, or at anyrate to as simple a form as it
can be brought to without our losing the sense of
its place in the world. The characters that are
involved in it are freed from everything that is not
a part of that action ; and whether it is, as in the
less important kinds of drama, a mere bodily activity,
a hair-breadth escape or the like, or as it is in the
more important kinds, an activity of the souls of the
characters, it is an energy, an eddy of life purified
from everything but itself. The dramatist must
picture life in action, with an unpreoccupied mind,

as the musician pictures her in sound and the sculptor in form.

But if this be true, has art nothing to do with moral judgments? Surely it has, and its judgments are those from which there is no appeal. The character, whose fortune we have been called in to see, or the personality of the writer, must keep our sympathy, and whether it be farce or tragedy, we must laugh and weep with him and call down blessings on his head. This character who delights us may commit murder like Macbeth, or fly the battle for his sweetheart as did Antony, or betray his country like Coriolanus, and yet we will rejoice in every happiness that comes to him and sorrow at his death as if it were our own. It is no use telling us that the murderer and the betrayer do not deserve our sympathy. We thought so yesterday, and we still know what crime is, but everything has been changed of a sudden; we are caught up into another code, we are in the presence of a higher court. Complain of us if you will, but it will be useless, for before the curtain falls a thousand ages, grown conscious in our sympathies, will have cried *Absolvo te*. Blame if you will the codes, the philosophies, the experiences of all past ages that have made us what we are, as the soil under our feet has been made out of unknown vegetations : quarrel with the acorns of Eden if you will, but what has that to do with us? We understand the verdict and not the law ; and yet there is some law, some code, some judgment. If the poet's hand had slipped, if Antony had railed at Cleopatra in the tower, if Coriolanus

had abated that high pride of his in the presence of
death, we might have gone away muttering the Ten
Commandments. Yet may be we are wrong to speak
of judgment, for we have but contemplated life, and
what more is there to say when she that is all virtue,
the gift and the giver, the fountain whither all flows
again, has given all herself? If the subject of drama
or any other art, were a man himself, an eddy of
momentary breath, we might desire the contemplation
of perfect characters ; but the subject of all art is
passion, the flame of life itself, and a passion can
only be contemplated when separated by itself,
purified of all but itself, and aroused into a perfect
intensity by opposition with some other passion, or it
may be with the law, that is the expression of the
whole whether of Church or Nation or external nature.
Had Coriolanus not been a law-breaker neither he
nor we had ever discovered, it may be, that noble
pride of his, and if we had not seen Cleopatra
through the eyes of so many lovers, would we have
known that soul of hers to be all flame, and wept at
the quenching of it ? If we were not certain of law
we would not feel the struggle, the drama, but the
subject of art is not law, which is a kind of death,
but the praise of life, and it has no commandments
that are not positive.

But if literature does not draw its substance from
history, or anything about us in the world, what is
a National literature? Our friends have already told
us, writers for the Theatre in Abbey Street, that we
have no right to the name, some because we do not
write in Irish, and others because we do not plead

the National cause in our plays, as if we were writers for the newspapers. I have not asked my fellow-workers what they mean by the words National literature, but though I have no great love for definitions, I would define it in some such way as this: It is the work of writers, who are moulded by influences that are moulding their country, and who write out of so deep a life that they are accepted there in the end. It leaves a good deal unsettled—was Rossetti an Englishman, or Swift an Irishman?—but it covers more kinds of National literature than any other I can think of. If one says a National literature must be in the language of the country, there are many difficulties. Should it be written in the language that one's country does speak or the language that it ought to speak? Was Milton an Englishman when he wrote in Latin or Italian, and had we no part in Columbanus when he wrote in Latin the beautiful sermon comparing life to a highway and to a smoke? And then there is Beckford, who is in every history of English literature, and yet his one memorable book, a story of Persia, was written in French.

Our theatre is of no great size, for though we know that if we write well we shall find acceptance among our countrymen in the end, we would think our emotions were on the surface if we found a ready welcome. Edgar Allan Poe and Walt Whitman are National writers of America, although the one had his first true acceptance in France and the other in England and Ireland. When I was a boy, six persons, who, alone out of the whole world it may be, believed

Walt Whitman a great writer, sent him a message of admiration, and of those names four were English and two Irish, my father's and Prof. Dowden's. It is only in our own day that America has begun to prefer him to Lowell, who is not a poet at all.

I mean by deep life that men must put into their writing the emotions and experiences that have been most important to themselves. If they say, 'I will write of Irish country people and make them charming and picturesque like those dear peasants my great grandmother used to put in the foreground of her water-colour paintings,' then they had better be satisfied with the word 'provincial.' If one condescends to one's material, if it is only what a popular novelist would call local colour, it is certain that one's real soul is somewhere else. Mr. Synge, upon the other hand, who is able to express his own finest emotions in those curious ironical plays of his, where, for all that, by the illusion of admirable art, everyone seems to be thinking and feeling as only countrymen could think and feel, is truly a National writer, as Burns was when he wrote finely and as Burns was not when he wrote *Highland Mary* and *The Cotter's Saturday Night.*

A writer is not less National because he shows the influence of other countries and of the great writers of the world. No nation, since the beginning of history, has ever drawn all its life out of itself. Even The Well of English Undefiled, the Father of English Poetry himself, borrowed his metres, and much of his way of looking at the world, from French writers, and it is possible that the influence of Italy was more powerful

M

among the Elizabethan poets than any literary influence out of England herself. Many years ago, when I was contending with Sir Charles Gavan Duffy over what seemed to me a too narrow definition of Irish interests, Professor York Powell either said or wrote to me that the creative power of England was always at its greatest when her receptive power was greatest. If Ireland is about to produce a literature that is important to her, it must be the result of the influences that flow in upon the mind of an educated Irishman to-day, and, in a greater degree, of what came into the world with himself. Gaelic can hardly fail to do a portion of the work, but one cannot say whether it may not be some French or German writer who will do most to make him an articulate man. If he really achieve the miracle, if he really make all that he has seen and felt and known a portion of his own intense nature, if he put it all into the fire of his energy, he need not fear being a stranger among his own people in the end. There never have been men more unlike an Englishman's idea of himself than Keats and Shelley, while Campbell, whose emotion came out of a shallow well, was very like that idea. We call certain minds creative because they are among the moulders of their nation and are not made upon its mould, and they resemble one another in this only—they have never been fore-known or fulfilled an expectation.

It is sometimes necessary to follow in practical matters some definition which one knows to have but a passing use. We, for instance, have always confined ourselves to plays upon Irish subjects, as if no others could be National literature. Our theatre inherits this limitation from previous movements, which

found it necessary and fruitful. Goldsmith and
Sheridan and Burke had become so much a part of
English life, were so greatly moulded by the move-
ments that were moulding England, that, despite
certain Irish elements that clung about them, we
could not think of them as more important to us than
any English writer of equal rank. Men told us that
we should keep our hold of them, as it were, for they
were a part of our glory; but we did not consider
our glory very important. We had no desire to turn
braggarts, and we did suspect the motives of our
advisers. Perhaps they had reasons, which were not
altogether literary, for thinking it might be well if
Irishmen of letters, in our day also, would turn their
faces to England. But what moved me always the
most, and I had something to do with forcing this
limitation upon our organisations, is that a new
language of expression would help to awaken a new
attitude in writers themselves, and that if our organi-
sations were satisfied to interpret a writer to his own
countrymen merely because he was of Irish birth, the
organisations would become a kind of trade union for
the helping of Irishmen to catch the ear of London
publishers and managers, and for upholding writers
who had been beaten by abler Englishmen. Let a
man turn his face to us, accepting the commercial
disadvantages that would bring upon him, and talk
of what is near to our hearts, Irish Kings and
Irish Legends and Irish Countrymen, and we would
find it a joy to interpret him. Our one philosophical
critic, Mr. John Eglinton, thinks we were very
arbitrary, and yet I would not have us enlarge our
practice. England and France, almost alone among

nations, have great works of literature which have taken their subjects from foreign lands, and even in France and England this is more true in appearance than reality. Shakespeare observed his Roman crowds in London, and saw, one doubts not, somewhere in his own Stratford, the old man that gave Cleopatra the asp. Somebody I have been reading lately finds the Court of Louis the Fourteenth in Phèdre and Andromaque. Even in France and England almost the whole prose fiction professes to describe the life of the country, often of the districts where its writers have lived, for, unlike a poem, a novel requires so much minute observation of the surface of life that a novelist who cares for the illusion of reality will keep to familiar things. A writer will indeed take what is most creative out of himself, not from observation, but experience, yet he must master a definite language, a definite symbolism of incident and scene. Flaubert explains the comparative failure of his Salammbô by saying 'one cannot frequent her.' He could create her soul, as it were, but he could not tell with certainty how it would express itself before Carthage fell to ruins. In the small nations which have to struggle for their National life, one finds that almost every creator, whether poet or novelist, sets all his stories in his own country. I do not recollect that Björnson ever wrote of any land but Norway, and Ibsen, though he lived in exile for many years, driven out by his countrymen, as he believed, carried the little seaboard towns of Norway everywhere in his imagination. So far as one can be certain of anything, one may be certain that Ireland with her long National struggle, her old literature, her unbounded folk-imagination, will, in so far as her literature is National at all, be more like Norway than England or France.

If Literature is but praise of life, if our writers are not to plead the National Cause, nor insist upon the Ten Commandments, nor upon the glory of their country, what part remains for it, in the common life of the country? It will influence the life of the country immeasurably more, though seemingly less, than have our propagandist poems and stories. It will leave to others the defence of all that can be codified for ready understanding, of whatever is the especial business of sermons, and of leading articles; but it will bring all the ways of men before that ancient tribunal of our sympathies. It will measure all things by the measure not of things visible but of things invisible. In a country like Ireland, where personifications have taken the place of life, men have more hate than love, for the unhuman is nearly the same as the inhuman, but literature, which is a part of that charity that is the forgiveness of sins, will make us understand men no matter how little they conform to our expectations. We will be more interested in heroic men than in heroic actions, and will have a little distrust for everything that can be called good or bad in itself with a very confident heart. Could we understand it so well, we will say, if it were not something other than human life? We will have a scale of virtues, and value most highly those that approach the indefinable. Men will be born among us of whom it is possible to say, not 'What a philanthropist,' 'What a patriot,' 'How practical a man,' but, as we say of the men of the Renaissance, 'What a nature,' 'How much abundant life.' Even at the beginning we will value qualities more than actions, for these may be habit or accident; and should we say to a friend, 'You have advertised for an English cook,' or 'I hear that you have no clerks who are not of your own faith,' or 'You have voted an address to the king,' we will add to our complaint, 'You have been unpatriotic and I am ashamed of you, but if you cease from doing any of these things because you have been terrorized out of them, you will cease to be my friend.' We will not forget how to be stern, but we will remember always that the highest life unites, as in one fire, the greatest passion and the greatest courtesy.

A feeling for the form of life, for the graciousness of life, for the dignity of life, for the moving limbs of life, for the nobleness of life, for all that cannot be written in codes, has always been greatest among the gifts of literature to mankind. Indeed, the Muses being women, all literature is but their love-cries to the manhood of the world. It is now one and now another that cries, but the words are the same—'Love of my heart, what matter to me that you have been quarrelsome in your cups, and have slain many, and have given your love here and there? It was because of the whiteness of your flesh and the mastery in your hands that I gave you my love, when all life came to me in your coming.' And then in a low voice that none may overhear—'Alas! I am greatly afraid that the more they cry against you the more I love you.'

There are two kinds of poetry, and they are co-
mingled in all the greatest works. When the tide
of life sinks low there are pictures, as in *The Ode
to a Grecian Urn* and in Virgil at the plucking of
the Golden Bough. The pictures make us sorrowful.
We share the poet's separation from what he describes.
It is life in the mirror, and our desire for it is as the
desire of the lost souls for God; but when Lucifer
stands among his friends, when Villon sings his dead
ladies to so gallant a rhythm, when Timon makes
his epitaph, we feel no sorrow, for life herself has
made one of her eternal gestures, has called up into
our hearts her energy that is eternal delight. In
Ireland, where the tide of life is rising, we turn,
not to picture-making, but to the imagination of
personality—to drama, gesture.

THE PLAY, THE PLAYER, AND THE SCENE.

I have been asked to put into this year's *Samhain* Miss Horniman's letter offering us the use of the Abbey Theatre. I have done this, but as Miss Horniman begins her letter by stating that she has made her offer out of 'great sympathy with the Irish National Theatre Company as publicly explained by Mr. Yeats on various occasions,' she has asked me to go more into detail as to my own plans and hopes than I have done before. I think they are the plans and hopes of my fellow dramatists, for we are all of one movement, and have influenced one another, and have in us the spirit of our time. I discussed them all very shortly in last *Samhain*. And I know that it was that *Samhain*, and a certain speech I made in front of the curtain, that made Miss Horniman entrust us with her generous gift. But last *Samhain* is practically out of print, and my speech has gone even out of my own memory. I will repeat, therefore, much that I have said already, but adding a good deal to it.

First. Our plays must be literature or written in the spirit of literature. The modern theatre has died away to what it is because the writers have thought of their audiences instead of their subject. An old writer saw his hero, if it was a play of character; or some dominant passion, if it was a play of passion, like Phèdre or Andromaque, moving before him, living with a life he did not endeavour to control. The persons acted upon one another as they were bound by their natures to act, and the play was dramatic, not because he had sought out dramatic situations for their own sake, but because will broke itself upon will and passion upon passion. Then the imagination began to cool, the writer began to be less alive, to seek external aids, remembered situations, tricks of the theatre, that had proved themselves again and again. His persons no longer will have a particular character, but he knows that he can rely upon the incidents, and he feels himself fortunate when there is nothing in his play that has not succeeded a thousand times before the curtain has risen. Perhaps he has even read a certain guide-book to the stage published in France, and called 'The Thirty-six Situations of Drama.' The costumes will be magnificent, the actresses will be beautiful, the Castle in Spain will be painted by an artist upon the spot. We will come from his play excited if we are foolish, or can condescend to the folly of others, but knowing nothing new about ourselves, and seeing life with no new eyes and hearing it with no new ears. The whole movement of theatrical reform in our day has been a struggle to get rid of this kind of play, and the sincere play, the logical play, that we would have in its place, will always seem, when we hear it for the first time, undramatic, unexciting. It has to stir the heart in a long disused way, it has to awaken the intellect to a pleasure that ennobles and wearies. I was at the first performance of an Ibsen play given in England. It was *The Doll's House*, and at the fall of the curtain I heard an old dramatic critic say, 'It is but a series of conversations terminated by an accident.' So far, we here in Dublin mean the same thing as do Mr. Max Beerbohm, Mr. Walkley, and Mr. Archer, who are seeking to restore sincerity to the English stage, but I am not certain that we mean the same thing all through. The utmost sincerity, the most unbroken logic, give me, at any rate, but an imperfect pleasure if there is not a vivid and beautiful language. Ibsen has sincerity and logic beyond any writer of our time, and we are all seeking to learn them at his hands; but is he not a good deal less than the greatest of all times, because he lacks beautiful and vivid language? 'Well, well, give me time and you shall hear all about it. If only I had Peter here now,' is very like life, is entirely in its place where it comes, and when it is united to other sentences exactly like itself, one is moved, one knows not how, to pity and terror, and yet not moved as if the words themselves could sing and shine. Mr. Max Beerbohm wrote once that a play cannot have style because the people must talk as they talk in daily life. He was thinking, it is obvious, of a play made out of that typically modern life where there is no longer vivid speech. Blake says that a work of art must be minutely articulated by God or man, and man has too little help from that occasional collaborateur when he writes of people whose language has become abstract and dead. Falstaff gives one the sensation of reality, and when one remembers the abundant vocabulary of a time when all but everything present to the mind was present to the senses, one imagines that his words were but little magnified from the words of such a man in real life: Language was still alive then, alive as it is in Gaelic to-day, as it is in English-speaking

Ireland where the Schoolmaster or the newspaper
has not corrupted it.   I know that we are at the
mere beginning, laboriously learning our craft, trying
our hands in little plays for the most part, that we
may not venture too boldly in our ignorance; but I
never hear the vivid, picturesque, ever-varied lan-
guage of Mr. Synge's persons without feeling that
the great collaborateur has his finger in our business.
May it not be that the only realistic play that will
live as Shakespeare has lived, as Calderon has lived, as
the Greeks have lived, will arise out of the common
life, where language is as much alive as if it were
new come out of Eden? After all, is not the greatest
play not the play that gives the sensation of an
external reality but the play in which there is the
greatest abundance of life itself, of the reality that is
in our minds?   Is it possible to make a work of art,
which needs every subtlety of expression if it is to
reveal what hides itself continually, out of a dying,
or at any rate a very ailing language? and all language
but that of the poets and of the poor is already bed-
ridden. We have, indeed, persiflage, the only speech
of educated men that expresses a deliberate enjoy-
ment of words: but persiflage is not a true language.
It is impersonal; it is not in the midst but on the
edge of life; it covers more character than it dis-
covers: and yet, such as it is, all our comedies are
made out of it.

What the ever-moving delicately-moulded flesh
is to human beauty, vivid musical words are to pas-
sion. Somebody has said that every nation begins
with poetry and ends with algebra, and passion has
always refused to express itself in algebraical terms.

Have we not been in error in demanding from our playwrights personages who do not transcend our common actions any more than our common speech? If we are in the right, all antiquity has been in error. The scholars of a few generations ago were fond of deciding that certain persons were unworthy of the dignity of art. They had, it may be, an over-abounding preference for kings and queens, but we are, it may be, very stupid in thinking that the average man is a fit subject at all for the finest art. Art delights in the exception, for it delights in the soul expressing itself according to its own laws and arranging the world about it in its own pattern, as sand strewn upon a drum will change itself into different patterns, according to the notes of music that are sung or played to it. But the average man is average because he has not attained to freedom. Habit, routine, fear of public opinion, fear of punishment here or hereafter, a myriad of things that are 'something other than human life,' something less than flame, work their will upon his soul and trundle his body here and there. At the first performance of *Ghosts* I could not escape from an illusion unaccountable to me at the time. All the characters seemed to be less than life-size ; the stage, though it was but the little Royalty stage, seemed larger than I had ever seen it. Little whimpering puppets moved here and there in the middle of that great abyss. Why did they not speak out with louder voices or move with freer gestures ? What was it that weighed upon their souls perpetually ? Certainly they were all in prison, and yet there was no prison. In India there are villages

so obedient that all the jailer has to do is to draw a
circle upon the ground with his staff, and to tell his
thief to stand there so many hours ; but what law
had these people broken that they had to wander
round that narrow circle all their lives ?   May not
such art, terrible, satirical, inhuman, be the medicine
of great cities, where nobody is ever alone with his
own strength ?   Nor is Maeterlinck very different,
for his persons 'enquire after Jerusalem in the
regions of the grave, with weak voices almost
inarticulate, wearying repose.'   Is it the mob that
has robbed those angelic persons of the energy of
their souls ?   Will not our next art be rather of the
country, of great open spaces, of the soul rejoicing
in itself?   Will not the generations to come begin
again to have an over-abounding faith in kings and
queens, in masterful spirits, whatever names we call
them by ?   I had Molière with me on my way to
America, and as I read I seemed to be at home in
Ireland listening to that conversation of the people
which is so full of riches because so full of leisure,
or to those old stories of the folk which were made
by men who believed so much in the soul, and so
little in anything else, that they were never entirely
certain that the earth was solid under the foot-sole.
What is there left for us, that have seen the newly-
discovered stability of things changed from an en-
thusiasm to a weariness, but to labour with a high
heart, though it may be with weak hands, to rediscover
an art of the theatre that shall be joyful, fantastic,
extravagant, whimsical, beautiful, resonant, and
altogether reckless ?   The arts are at their greatest
when they seek for a life growing always more

scornful of everything that is not itself and passing
into its own fulness, as it were, ever more completely,
as all that is created out of the passing mode of
society slips from it; and attaining that fulness,
perfectly it may be—and from this is tragic joy and
the perfectness of tragedy—when the world itself
has slipped away in death. We, who are believers,
cannot see reality anywhere but in the soul itself,
and seeing it there we cannot do other than rejoice
in every energy, whether of gesture, or of action, or
of speech, coming out of the personality, the soul's
image, even though the very laws of nature seem as
unimportant in comparison as did the laws of Rome
to Coriolanus when his pride was upon him. Has
not the long decline of the arts been but the shadow
of declining faith in an unseen reality?

> 'If the sun and moon would doubt,
> They 'd immediately go out.'

Second. If we are to make a drama of energy, of
extravagance, of phantasy, of musical and noble
speech, we shall need an appropriate stage manage-
ment. Up to a generation or two ago, and to our
own generation, here and there, lingered a method
of acting and of stage-management, which had come
down, losing much of its beauty and meaning on the
way, from the days of Shakespeare. Long after
England, under the influence of Garrick, began the
movement towards Naturalism, this school had a
great popularity in Ireland, where it was established
at the Restoration by an actor who probably re-
membered the Shakespearean players. France has
inherited from Racine and from Molière an equivalent

art, and, whether it is applied to comedy or to tragedy,
its object is to give importance to the words. It is
not only Shakespeare whose finest thoughts are
inaudible on the English stage. Congreve's *Way
of the World* was acted in London last Spring, and
revived again a month ago, and the part of Lady
Wishfort was taken by a very admirable actress, an
actress of genius who has never had the recognition
she deserves. There is a scene where Lady Wishfort
turns away a servant with many words. She cries—
' Go, set up for yourself again, do; drive a trade, do,
with your three pennyworth of small ware, flaunting
upon a packthread under a brandy-seller's bulk, or
against a dead wall by a ballad-monger; go, hang
out an old frisoneer-gorget, with a yard of yellow
colberteen again, do; an old gnawed mask, two
rows of pins, and a child's fiddle ; a glass necklace
with the beads broken, and a quilted nightcap with
one ear. Go, go, drive a trade.' The conversation
of an older time, of Urquhart, the translator of
Rabelais, let us say, awakes with a little of its old
richness. The actress acted so much and so admirably
that when she first played it—I heard her better a
month ago, perhaps because I was nearer to the
stage—I could not understand a word of a passage
that required the most careful speech. Just as the
modern musician, through the over-development of
an art that seems exterior to the poet, writes so many
notes for every word that the natural energy of
speech is dissolved and broken and the words made
inaudible, so did this actress, a perfect mistress of
her own art, put into her voice so many different
notes, so run up and down the scale under an impulse

of anger and scorn, that one had hardly been more affronted by a musical setting. Everybody who has spoken to large audiences knows that he must speak difficult passages, in which there is some delicacy of sound or of thought, upon one or two notes. The larger his audience, the more he must get away, except in trivial passages, from the methods of conversation. Where one requires the full attention of the mind, one must not weary it with any but the most needful changes of pitch and note, or by an irrelevant or obtrusive gesture. As long as drama was full of poetical beauty, full of description, full of philosophy, as long as its words were the very vesture of sorrow and laughter, the players understood that their art was essentially conventional, artificial, ceremonious.

The stage itself was differently shaped, being more a platform than a stage, for they did not desire to picture the surface of life, but to escape from it. But realism came in, and every change towards realism coincided with a decline in dramatic energy. The proscenium was imported into England at the close of the seventeenth century, appropriate costumes a generation later. The audience were forbidden to sit upon the stage in the time of Sheridan, the last English-speaking playwright whose plays have lived. And the last remnant of the platform, the part of the stage that still projected beyond the proscenium, dwindled in size till it disappeared in their own day. The birth of science was at hand, the birth-pangs of its mother had troubled the world for centuries. But now that Gargantua is born at last, it may be possible to remember that there are other giants.

We can never bring back old things precisely as they were, but must consider how much of them is necessary to us, accepting, even if it were only out of politeness, something of our own time. The necessities of a builder have torn from us, all unwilling as we were, the apron, as the portion of the platform that came in front of the proscenium used to be called, and we must submit to the picture-making of the modern stage. We would have preferred to be able to return occasionally to the old stage of statue-making, of gesture. On the other hand, one accepts, believing it to be a great improvement, some appropriateness of costume, but speech is essential to us. An Irish critic has told us to study the stage-management of Antoine, but that is like telling a good Catholic to take his theology from Luther. Antoine, who described poetry as a way of saying nothing, has perfected naturalistic acting and carried the spirit of science into the theatre. Were we to study his methods, we might, indeed, have a far more perfect art than our own, a far more mature art, but it is better to fumble our way like children. We may grow up, for we have as good hopes as any other sturdy ragamuffin.

An actor must so understand how to discriminate cadence from cadence, and so cherish the musical lineaments of verse or prose, that he delights the ear with a continually varied music. This one has to say over and over again, but one does not mean that his speaking should be a monotonous chant. Those who have heard Mr. Frank Fay speaking verse will understand me. That speech of his, so masculine and so musical, could only sound monotous to an ear that was deaf to poetic rhythm, and one should never, as do London managers, stage a poetical drama according to the desire of those who are deaf to poetical rhythm. It is possible, barely so, but still possible, that some day we may write musical notes as did the Greeks, it seems, for a whole play, and make our actors speak upon them—not sing, but speak. Even now, when one wishes to make the voice immortal and passionless, as in the Angel's part in my *Hour-Glass*, one finds it desirable for the player to speak always upon pure musical notes, written out beforehand and carefully rehearsed. On the one occasion when I heard the Angel's part spoken in this way with entire success, the contrast between the crystalline quality of the pure notes and the more confused and passionate speaking of the Wise Man was a new dramatic effect of great value.

If a song is brought into a play it does not matter to what school the musician belongs if every word, if every cadence, is as audible and expressive as if it were spoken. It must be good speech, and one must not listen to the musician if he promise to add meaning to the words with his notes, for one does not add meaning to the word 'love' by putting four o's in the middle, or by subordinating it even slightly to a musical note. But where will one find a musician so mild, so quiet, so modest, unless he be a sailor from the forecastle or some ghost out of the twelfth century? One must ask him for music that shall mean nothing, or next to nothing, apart from the words, and after all he is a musician.

When I heard the Æschylean Trilogy at Stratford-on-Avon last spring I could not hear a word of the chorus, except in a few lines here and there which were spoken without musical setting. The chorus was not without dramatic, or rather operatic effect; but why should those singers have taken so much trouble to learn by heart so much of the greatest lyric poetry of Greece? 'Twinkle, twinkle, little star,' or any other memory of their childhood, would have served their turn. If it had been comic verse, the singing-master and the musician would have respected it, and the audience would have been able to hear. Mr. Dolmetsch and Miss Florence Farr have been working for some time to find out some way of setting serious poetry which will enable us to hear it, and the singer to sing sweetly and yet never to give a word, a cadence, or an accent, that would not be given it in ordinary passionate speech. It is difficult, for they are trying to re-discover an art that is only remembered or half-remembered in ships and in hovels and among wandering tribes of uncivilised men, and they have to make their experiment with singers who have been trained by a method of teaching that professes to change a human being into a musical instrument, a creation of science, 'something other than human life.' In old days the singer began to sing over the rocking cradle or among the wine-cups, and it was as though life itself caught fire of a sudden; but to-day the poet, fanatic that he is, watches the singer go up on to the platform, wondering and expecting every moment that he will punch himself as if he were a bag. It is certainly impossible to speak with perfect expression after you have been a bagpipes for many years, even though you have been making the most beautiful music all the time.

The success of the chorus in the performance of *Hippolytus* last Spring—I did not see the more recent performance, but hear upon all hands that the chorus was too large—the expressiveness of the greater portion as mere speech, has, I believe, re-created the chorus as a dramatic method. The greater portion of the singing, as arranged by Miss Farr, even when four or five voices sang together, though never when ten sang together, was altogether admirable speech, and some of it was speech of extraordinary beauty. When one lost the meaning, even perhaps where the whole chorus sang together, it was not because of a defective method, but because it is the misfortune of every new artistic method that we can only judge of it through performers who must be for a long time unpractised and amateurish. This new art has a double difficulty, for the training of a modern singer makes articulate speech, as a poet understands it, nearly impossible, and those who are masters of speech very often, perhaps usually, are poor musicians. Fortunately, Miss Farr, who has some knowledge of music, has, it may be, the most beautiful voice on the English stage, and is in her management of it an exquisite artist.

That we may throw emphasis on the words in poetical drama, above all where the words are remote from real life as well as in themselves exacting and difficult, the actors must move, for the most part, slowly and quietly, and not very much, and there should be something in their movements decorative and rhythmical as if they were paintings on a frieze. They must not draw attention to themselves at wrong moments, for poetry and indeed all picturesque writing is perpetually making little pictures which draw the attention away for a second or two from the player.   The actress who played Lady Wishfort should have permitted us to give a part of our attention to that little shop or wayside booth.   Then, too, one must be content to have long quiet moments, long grey spaces, long level reaches, as it were—the leisure that is in all fine life—for what we may call the business-will in a high state of activity is not everything, although contemporary drama knows of little else.

Third. We must have a new kind of scenic art. I have been the advocate of the poetry as against the actor, but I am the advocate of the actor as against the scenery.   Ever since the last remnant of the old platform disappeared, and the proscenium grew into the frame of a picture, the actors have been turned into a picturesque group in the foreground of a meretricious landscape-painting.   The background should be of as little importance as the background of a portrait-group, and it should, when possible, be of one colour or of one tint, that the persons on the stage, wherever they stand, may harmonise with it or contrast with it and preoccupy our attention.   Their outline should be clear and not broken up into the outline of windows and wainscotting, or lost into the edges of colours.   In a play which copies the surface of life in its dialogue one may, with this reservation, represent anything that can be represented successfully—a room, for instance—but a landscape painted in the ordinary way will always be meretricious and vulgar.   It will always be an attempt to do something which cannot be done successfully except in easel painting, and the moment an actor stands near to your mountain, or your forest, one will perceive that he is standing against a flat surface. Illusion, therefore, is impossible, and should not be attempted. One should be content to suggest a scene upon a canvas, whose vertical flatness one accepts and uses, as the decorator of pottery accepts the roundness of a bowl or a jug. Having chosen the distance from naturalism, which will keep one's composition from competing with the illusion created by the actor, who belongs to a world with depth as well as height and breadth, one must keep this distance without flinching. The distance will vary according to the distance the playwright has chosen, and especially in poetry, which is more remote and idealistic than prose, one will insist on schemes of colour and simplicity of form, for every sign of deliberate order gives remoteness and ideality. But, whatever the distance be, one's treatment will always be more or less decorative. We can only find out the right decoration for the different types of play by experiment, but it will probably range between, on the one hand, woodlands made out of recurring pattern, or painted like old religious pictures upon gold background, and upon the other the comparative realism of a Japanese print. This decoration will not only give us a scenic art that will be a true art because peculiar to the stage, but it will give the imagination liberty, and without returning to the bareness of the Elizabethan stage. The poet cannot evoke a picture to the mind's eye if a second-rate painter has set his imagination of it before the bodily eye; but decoration and suggestion will accompany our moods, and turn our minds to meditation, and yet never become obtrusive or wearisome. The actor and the words put into his mouth are always the one thing that matters, and the scene should never be complete of itself, should never mean anything to the imagination until the actor is in front of it.

If one remembers that the movement of the actor, and the graduation and the colour of the lighting, are the two elements that distinguish the stage picture from an easel painting, one will not find it difficult to create an art of the stage ranking as a true fine art. Mr. Gordon Craig has done wonderful things with the lighting, but he is not greatly interested in the actor, and his streams of coloured direct light, beautiful as they are, will always seem, apart from certain exceptional moments, a new externality. One should rather desire, for all but exceptional moments, an even, shadowless light, like that of noon, and it may be that a light reflected out of mirrors will give us what we need.

M. Appia and M. Fortuni are making experiments in the staging of Wagner for a private theatre in Paris, but I cannot understand what M. Appia is doing, from the little I have seen of his writing, excepting that the floor of the stage will be uneven like the ground, and that at moments the lights and shadows of green boughs will fall over the player that the stage may show a man wandering through a wood, and not a wood with a man in the middle of it. One agrees with all the destructive part of his criticism, but it looks as if he himself is seeking, not convention, but a more perfect realism. I cannot persuade myself that the movement of life is flowing that way, for life moves by a throbbing as of a pulse, by reaction and action. The hour of convention and decoration and ceremony is coming again.

The experiments of the Irish National Theatre Society will have of necessity to be for a long time few and timid, and we must often, having no money and not a great deal of leisure, accept for a while compromises, and much even that we know to be irredeemably bad. One can only perfect an art very gradually; and good playwriting, good speaking, and good acting are the first necessity.

1905

Our first season at the Abbey Theatre has been tolerably successful. We drew small audiences, but quite as big as we had hoped for, and we end the year with a little money. On the whole we have probably more than trebled our audiences of the Molesworth Hall. The same people come again and again, and others join them, and I do not think we lose any of them. We shall be under more expense in our new season, for we have decided to pay some of the company and send them into the provinces, but our annual expenses will not be as heavy as the weekly expenses of the most economical London manager. Mr. Philip Carr, whose revivals of Elizabethan plays and old comedies have been the finest things one could see in a London theatre, spent three hundred pounds and took twelve pounds during his last week; but here in Ireland enthusiasm can do half the work, and nobody is accustomed to get much money, and even Mr. Carr's inexpensive scenery costs more than our simple decorations. Our staging of *Kincora*, the work of Mr. Robert Gregory, was beautiful, with a high, grave dignity and that strangeness which Ben Jonson thought to be a part of all excellent beauty, and the expense of scenery, dresses and all was hardly above thirty pounds. If we find a good scene we repeat it in other plays, and in course of time we shall be able to put on new plays without any expense for scenery at all. I do not think that even the most expensive decoration would increase in any way the pleasure of an audience that comes to us for the play and the acting.

We shall have abundance of plays, for Lady Gregory has written us a new comedy besides her *White Cockade*, which is in rehearsal; Mr. Boyle, a satirical comedy in three acts; Mr. Colum has made a new play out of his *Broken Soil*; and I have made almost a new one out of my *Shadowy Waters*; and Mr. Synge has practically finished a longer and more elaborate comedy than his last. Since our start last Christmas we have shown eleven plays created by our movement and very varied in substance and form, and six of these were new: *The Well of the Saints*, *Kincora*, *The Building Fund*, *The Land*, *On Baile's Strand*, and *Spreading the News*.

One of our plays, *The Well of the Saints*, has been accepted for immediate production by the Deutsches Theatre of Berlin; and another, *The Shadow of the Glen*, is to be played during the season at the National Bohemian Theatre at Prague; and my own *Cathleen ni Houlihan* has been translated into Irish and been played at the Oireachtas, before an audience of some thousands. We have now several dramatists who have taken to drama as their most serious business, and we claim that a school of Irish drama exists, and that it is founded upon sincere observation and experience.

As is natural in a country where the Gaelic League has created a pre-occupation with the countryman, the greatest number of our plays are founded on the comedy and tragedy of country life, and are written more or less in dialect. When the Norwegian

National movement began, its writers chose for their
maxim, 'To understand the saga by the peasant and
the peasant by the saga.' Ireland in our day has re-
discovered the old heroic literature of Ireland, and
she has re-discovered the imagination of the folk.
My own pre-occupation is more with the heroic
legend than with the folk, but Lady Gregory in her
Spreading the News, Mr. Synge in his *Well of the Saints*,
Mr. Colum in *The Land*, Mr. Boyle in *The Building
Fund*, have been busy, much or little, with the folk
and the folk-imagination.   Mr. Synge alone has
written of the peasant as he is to all the ages; of the
folk-imagination as it has been shaped by centuries
of life among fields or on fishing-grounds.   His
people talk a highly-coloured musical language, and
one never hears from them a thought that is of to-day
and not of yesterday.   Lady Gregory has written of
the people of the markets and villages of the West,
and their speech, though less full of peculiar idiom
than that of Mr. Synge's people, is still always that
vivid speech which has been shaped through some
generations of English speaking by those who still
think in Gaelic.   Mr. Colum and Mr. Boyle, on the
other hand, write of the countryman or villager of
the East or centre of Ireland, who thinks in English,
and the speech of their people shows the influence
of the newspaper and the National Schools.   The
people they write of, too, are not the true folk.
They are the peasant as he is being transformed by
modern life, and for that very reason the man of the
towns may find it easier to understand them.   There
is less surprise, less wonder in what he sees, but there
is more of himself there, more of his vision of the
world and of the problems that are troubling him.

It is not fitting for the showman to overpraise the show, but he is always permitted to tell you what is in his booths. Mr. Synge is the most obviously individual of our writers. He alone has discovered a new kind of sarcasm, and it is this sarcasm that keeps him, and may long keep him, from general popularity. Mr. Boyle satirises a miserly old woman, and he has made a very vivid person of her, but as yet his satire is such as all men accept; it brings no new thing to judgment. We have never doubted that what he assails is evil, and we are never afraid that it is ourselves. Lady Gregory alone writes out of a spirit of pure comedy, and laughs without bitterness and with no thought but to laugh. She has a perfect sympathy with her characters, even with the worst of them, and when the curtain goes down we are so far from the mood of judgment that we do not even know that we have condoned many sins. In Mr. Colum's *Land* there is a like comedy when Cornelius and Sally fill the scene, but then he is too young to be content with laughter. He is still interested in the reform of society, but that will pass, for at about thirty every writer, who is anything of an artist, comes to understand that all a work of art can do is to show one the reality that is within our minds, and the reality that our eyes look on. He is the youngest of us all by many years, and we are all proud to foresee his future.

I think that a race or a nation or a phase of life has but few dramatic themes, and that when these have been once written well they must afterwards be written less and less well until one gets at last but

'Soulless self-reflections of man's skill.' The first
man writes what it is natural to write, the second
man what is left to him, for the imagination cannot
repeat itself. The hoydenish young woman, the
sentimental young woman, the villain and the hero
alike ever self-possessed, of contemporary drama,
were once real discoveries, and one can trace their
history through the generations like a joke or a folk-
tale, but, unlike these, they grow always less inter-
esting as they get farther from their cradle. Our
opportunity in Ireland is not that our playwrights
have more talent, it is possible that they have less
than the workers in an old tradition, but that the
necessity of putting a life that has not hitherto been
dramatised into their plays excludes all these types
which have had their origin in a different social
order.

An audience with National feeling is alive, at the
worst it is alive enough to quarrel with. One man
came up from the scene of Lady Gregory's *Kincora*
at Killaloe that he might see her play, and having
applauded loudly, and even cheered for the Dal-
cassians, became silent and troubled when Brian took
Gormleith for his wife. 'It is a great pity,' he said
to a man next to him, 'that he didn't marry a quiet
girl from his own district.' Some have quarrelled with
me because I did not take some glorious moment of
Cuchulain's life for my play, and not the killing of
his son, and all our playwrights have been attacked
for choosing bad characters instead of good, and called
slanderers of their country. In so far as these attacks
come from National feeling, that is to say, out of an
interest or an affection for the life of this country

now and in past times, as did the countryman's
trouble about Gormleith, they are in the long run
the greatest help to a dramatist, for they give him
something to startle or to delight. Every writer has
had to face them where his work has aroused a genuine
interest. The Germans at the beginning of the nine-
teenth century preferred Schiller to Goethe, and
thought him the greater writer, because he put nobler
characters into his books; and when Chaucer met
Eros walking in the month of May, that testy god
complains that though he had 'sixty bookkes olde
and newe,' and all full of stories of women and the
life they led, and though for every bad woman there
are a hundred good, he has chosen to write only of
the bad ones. He complains that Chaucer by his
Troilus and his *Romaunt of the Rose* has brought love
and women to discredit. It is the same in painting
as in literature, for when a new painter arises men
cry out, even when he is a painter of the beautiful
like Rossetti, that he has chosen the exaggerated or
the ugly or the unhealthy, forgetting that it is the
business of art and of letters to change the values and
to mint the coinage. Without this outcry there is
no movement of life in the arts, for it is the sign of
values not yet understood, of a coinage not yet mas-
tered. Sometimes the writer delights us, when we
grow to understand him, with new forms of virtue
discovered in persons where one had not hitherto
looked for it, and sometimes, and this is more and
more true of modern art, he changes the values not
by the persons he sets before one, who may be mean
enough, but by his way of looking at them, by the
implications that come from his own mind, by the

tune they dance to as it were. Eros, into whose mouth Chaucer, one doubts not, puts arguments that he had heard from his readers and listeners, objected to Chaucer's art in the interests of pedantic mediæval moralising; the contemporaries of Schiller commended him for reflecting vague romantic types from the sentimental literature of his predecessors; and those who object to the peasant as he is seen in the Abbey Theatre have their imaginations full of what is least observant and most sentimental in the Irish novelists. When I was a boy I spent many an afternoon with a village shoemaker who was a great reader. I asked him once what Irish novels he liked, and he told me there were none he could read, 'They sentimentalised the people,' he said angrily; and it was against Kickham that he complained most. 'I want to see the people,' he said, 'shown up in their naked hideousness.' That is the peasant mind as I know it, delight in strong sensations whether of beauty or of ugliness, in bare facts, and quite without sentimentality. The sentimental mind is the bourgeois mind, and it was this mind which came into Irish literature with Gerald Griffin and later on with Kickham.

It is the mind of the town, and it is a delight to those only who have seen life, and above all country life, with unobservant eyes, and most of all to the Irish tourist, to the patriotic young Irishman who goes to the country for a month's holiday with his head full of vague idealisms. It is not the art of Mr. Colum, born of the people, and when at his best looking at the town and not the country with strange eyes, nor the art of Mr. Synge spending weeks and months in remote places talking Irish to fishers and islanders. I remember meeting, about twenty years ago, a lad who had a little yacht at Kingstown. Somebody was talking of the sea paintings of a great painter, Hook, I think, and this made him very angry. No yachtsman believed in them or thought them at all like the sea, he said. Indeed, he was always hearing people praise pictures that were not a bit like the sea, and thereupon he named certain of the greatest painters of water— men who more than all others had spent their lives in observing the effects of light upon cloud and wave. I met him again the other day, well on in middle life, and though he is not even an Irishman, indignant with Mr. Synge's and Mr. Boyle's* peasants. He knew the people, he said, and neither he nor any other person that knew them could believe that they were properly represented in *The Well of the Saints* or *The Building Fund*. Twenty years ago his imagination was under the influence of popular pictures, but to-day it was under the conventional idealisms which writers like Kickham and Griffin substitute for the ever-varied life of the cottages, and that conventional idealism that the contemporary English Theatre substitutes for all life whatsoever. I saw *Caste*, the earliest play of the modern school, a few days ago, and found there more obviously than I expected, for I am not much of a theatre-goer, the English half of the mischief. Two of the minor persons had a certain amount of superficial characterization, as if out of the halfpenny comic papers;

* Mr. Boyle has since left us as a protest against the performance of Mr. Synge's *Playboy of the Western World*.—W.B.Y., *March*, 1908.

but the central persons, the man and woman that
created the dramatic excitement, such as it was, had
not characters of any kind, being vague ideals, per-
fection as it is imagined by a common-place mind.
The audience could give them its sympathy without
the labour that comes from awakening knowledge.
If the dramatist had put any man and woman of his
acquaintance that seemed to him nearest perfection
into his play, he would have had to make it a study,
among other things, of the little petty faults and
perverted desires that come out of the nature or its
surroundings. He would have troubled that admiring
audience by making a self-indulgent sympathy more
difficult.   He might have even seemed, like Ibsen
or the early Christians, an enemy of the human race.
We have gone down to the roots, and we have made
up our minds upon one thing quite definitely—that
in no play that professes to picture life in its daily
aspects shall we admit these white phantoms.   We
can do this, not because we have any special talent,
but because we are dealing with a life which has for
all practical purposes never been set upon the stage
before.   The conventional types of the novelists do
not pervert our imagination, for they are built, as it
were, into another form, and no man who has chosen
for himself a sound method of drama, whether it be
the drama of character or of crisis, can use them.
The Gaelic League and *Cumann na nGaedheal* play
does indeed show the influence of the novelists; but
the typical Gaelic League play is essentially narrative
and not dramatic.   Every artist necessarily imitates
those who have worked in the same form before him,
and when the preoccupation has been with the same

o

life he almost always, consciously or unconsciously, borrows more than the form, and it is this very borrowing—affecting thought, language, all the vehicles of expression—which brings about the most of what we call decadence.

After all, if our plays are slanders upon their country ; if to represent upon the stage a hard old man like Cosgar, or a rapacious old man like Shan, or a faithless wife like Nora Burke, or to select from history treacherous Gormleith for a theme, is to represent this nation at something less than its full moral worth ; if every play played in the Abbey Theatre now and in times to come be something of a slander, is anybody a penny the worse ? Some ancient or mediæval races did not think so. Jusserand describes the French conquerors of mediæval England as already imagining themselves in their literature, as they have done to this day, as a great deal worse than they are, and the English imagining themselves a great deal better. The greater portion of the *Divine Comedy* is a catalogue of the sins of Italy, and Boccaccio became immortal because he exaggerated with an unceasing playful wit the vices of his countryside. The Greeks chose for the themes of their serious literature a few great crimes, and Corneille, in his article on the theory of the drama, shows why the greatness and notoriety of these crimes is necessary to tragic drama. The public life of Athens found its chief celebration in the monstrous caricature of Aristophanes, and the Greek nation was so proud, so free from morbid sensitiveness, that it invited the foreign ambassadors to the spectacle.

And I answer to those who say that Ireland cannot
afford this freedom because of her political circum-
stances, that if Ireland cannot afford it, Ireland cannot
have a literature.   Literature has never been the
work of slaves, and Ireland must learn to say—

> 'Stone walls do not a prison make,
>   Nor iron bars a cage.'

The misrepresentation of the average life of a
nation that follows of necessity from an imaginative
delight in energetic characters and extreme types,
enlarges the energy of a people by the spectacle of
energy.   A nation is injured by the picking out of
a single type and setting that into print or upon the
stage as a type of the whole nation.   Ireland suffered
in this way from that single whisky-drinking,
humorous type which seemed for a time the accepted
type of all.   The Englishwoman is, no doubt, injured
in the same way in the minds of various Continental
nations by a habit of caricaturing all Englishwomen
as having big teeth.   But neither nation can be
injured by imaginative writers selecting types that
please their fancy.   They will never impose a general
type on the public mind, for genius differs from the
newspapers in this, that the greater and more con-
fident it is, the more is its delight in varieties and
species.   If Ireland were at this moment, through a
misunderstanding terror of the stage Irishman, to
deprive her writers of freedom, to make their
imaginations timid, she would lower her dignity in
her own eyes and in the eyes of every intellectual
nation.   That old caricature did her very little harm
in the long run, perhaps a few car-drivers have copied

it in their lives, while the mind of the country remained untroubled ; but the loss of imaginative freedom and daring would turn us into old women. In the long run, it is the great writer of a nation that becomes its image in the minds of posterity, and even though he represent no man of worth in his art, the worth of his own mind becomes the inheritance of his people. He takes nothing away that he does not give back in greater volume.

If Ireland had not lost the Gaelic she never would have had this sensitiveness as of a *parvenu* when presented at Court for the first time, or of a nigger newspaper. When Ireland had the confidence of her own antiquity, her writers praised and blamed according to their fancy, and even as throughout all mediæval Europe, they laughed when they had a mind to at the most respected persons, at the sanctities of Church and State. The story of *The Shadow of the Glen*, found by Mr. Synge in Gaelic-speaking Aran, and by Mr. Curtain in Munster ; the Song of *The Red-haired Man's Wife*, sung in all Gaelic Ireland ; *The Midnight Court of MacGiolla Meidhre* ; *The Vision of MacCoinglinne* ; the old romancers, with their Bricriu and their Conan, laughed and sang as fearlessly as Chaucer or Villon or Cervantes. It seemed almost as if those old writers murmured to themselves: 'If we but keep our courage let all the virtues perish, for we can make them over again; but if that be gone, all is gone.' I remember when I was an art student at the Metropolitan School of Art a good many years ago, saying to Mr. Hughes the sculptor, as we looked at the work of our fellow-students, 'Every student here that is doing better work than another is doing it because he has a more intrepid imagination; one has only to look at the line of a drawing to see that'; and he said that was his own thought also. All good art is extravagant, vehement, impetuous, shaking the dust of time from its feet, as it were, and beating against the walls of the world.

If a sincere religious artist were to arise in Ireland in our day, and were to paint the Holy Family, let us say, he would meet with the same opposition that sincere dramatists are meeting with to-day. The bourgeois mind is never sincere in the arts, and one finds in Irish chapels, above all in Irish convents, the religious art that it understands. A Connaught convent a little time ago refused a fine design for stained glass, because of the personal life in the faces and in the attitudes, which seemed to them ugly, perhaps even impious. They sent to the designer an insipid German chromo-lithograph, full of faces without expression or dignity, and gestures without personal distinction, and the designer, too anxious for success to reject any order, has carried out this ignoble design in glass of beautiful colour and quality. Let us suppose that Meister Stefan were to paint in Ireland to-day that exquisite Madonna of his, with her lattice of roses; a great deal that is said of our plays would be said of that picture. Why select for his model a little girl selling newspapers in the streets, why slander with that miserable little body the Mother of God? He could only answer, as the imaginative artist always answers, 'That is the way I have seen her in my mind, and what I have made of her is very living.' All art is founded upon personal vision, and the greater the art the more surprising the vision; and all bad art is founded upon impersonal types and images, accepted by average men and women out of imaginative poverty and timidity, or the exhaustion that comes from labour.

Nobody can force a movement of any kind to take any prearranged pattern to any very great extent; one can, perhaps, modify it a little, and that is all. When one says that it is going to develop in a certain way, one means that one sees, or imagines that one sees, certain energies which left to themselves are bound to give it a certain form. Writing in *Samhain* some years ago, I said that our plays would be of two kinds, plays of peasant life and plays of a romantic and heroic life, such as one finds in the folk-tales. To-day I can see other forces, and can foretell, I think, the form of technique that will arise. About fifty years ago, perhaps not so many, the playwrights of every country in the world became persuaded that their plays must reflect the surface of life; and the author of *Caste*, for instance, made a reputation by putting what seemed to be average common life and average common speech for the first time upon the stage in England, and by substituting real loaves of bread and real cups of tea for imaginary ones. He was not a very clever nor a very well-educated man, and he made his revolution superficially; but in other countries men of intellect and knowledge created that intellectual drama of real life, of which Ibsen's later plays are the ripened fruit. This change coincided with the substitution of science for religion in the conduct of life, and is, I believe, as temporary, for the practice of twenty centuries will surely take the sway in the end. A rhetorician in that novel of Petronius, which satirises, or perhaps one should say celebrates, Roman decadence, complains that the young people of his day are made blockheads by learning old romantic tales in the schools, instead of what belongs to common life. And yet is it not the romantic tale, the extravagant and ungovernable dream which comes out of youth; and is not that desire for what belongs to common life, whether it comes from Rome or Greece or England, the sign. of fading fires, of ebbing imaginative desire ? In the arts I am quite certain that it is a substitution of apparent for real truth. Mr. George Moore has a very vivid character; he is precisely one of those whose characters can be represented most easily upon the stage. Let us suppose that some dramatist had made even him the centre of a play in which the moderation of common life was carefully preserved, how very little he could give us of that headlong intrepid man, as we know him, whether through long personal knowledge or through his many books. The more carefully the play reflected the surface of life the more would the elements be limited to those that naturally display themselves during so many minutes of our ordinary affairs. It is only by extravagance, by an emphasis far greater than that of life as we observe it, that we can crowd into a few minutes the knowledge of years. Shakespeare or Sophocles can so quicken, as it were, the circles of the clock, so heighten the expression of life, that many years can unfold themselves in a few minutes, and it is always Shakespeare or Sophocles, and not Ibsen, that makes us say, 'How true, how often I have felt as that man feels'; or 'How intimately I have come to know those people on the stage.' There is a certain school of painters that has discovered that it is necessary in the representation of light to put little touches of pure colour side by side. When you went up close to that big picture of the Alps by Segantini, in Mr. Lane's Loan Exhibition a year ago, you found that the grass seeds, which looked brown enough from the other side of the room, were full of pure scarlet colour. If you copy nature's moderation of colour you do not imitate her, for you have only white paint and she has light. If you wish to represent character or passion upon the stage, as it is known to the friends, let us say, of your principal persons, you must be excessive, extravagant, fantastic even, in expression; and you must be this, more extravagantly, more excessively, more fantastically than ever, if you wish to show character and passion as they would be known to the principal person of your play in the depths of his own mind. The greatest art symbolises not those things that we have observed so much as those things that we have experienced, and when the imaginary saint or lover or hero moves us most deeply, it is the moment when he awakens within us for an instant our own heroism, our own sanctity, our own desire. We possess these things—the greatest of men not more than Seaghan the Fool—not at all moderately, but to an infinite extent, and though we control or ignore them, we know that the moralists speak true when they compare them to angels or to devils, or to beasts of prey. How can any dramatic art, moderate in expression, be a true image of hell or heaven or the wilderness, or do anything but create those faint histories that but touch our curiosity, those groups of persons that never follow us into our intimate life, where Odysseus and Don Quixote and Hamlet are with us always?

The scientific movement is ebbing a little everywhere, and here in Ireland it has never been in flood at all. And I am certain that everywhere literature will return once more to its old extravagant fantastical expression, for in literature, unlike science, there are no discoveries, and it is always the old that returns. Everything in Ireland urges us to this return, and it may be that we shall be the first to recover after the fifty years of mistake.

The antagonism of imaginative writing in Ireland is not a habit of scientific observation but our interest in matters of opinion. A misgoverned country seeking a remedy by agitation puts an especial value upon opinion, and even those who are not conscious of any interest in the country are influenced by the general habit. All fine literature is the disinterested contemplation or expression of life, but hardly any Irish writer can liberate his mind sufficiently from questions of practical reform for this contemplation. Art for art's sake, as he understands it, whether it be the art of the *Ode to a Grecian Urn* or of the imaginer of Falstaff, seems to him a neglect of public duty. It is as though the telegraph-boys botanised among the hedges with the undelivered envelopes in their pockets; one must calculate the effect of one's words

before one writes them, who they are to excite and to
what end. We all write if we follow the habit of the
country not for our own delight but for the improve-
ment of our neighbours, and this is not only true of
such obviously propagandist work as *The Spirit of the
Nation* or a Gaelic League play, but of the work of
writers who seemed to have escaped from every
national influence, like Mr. Bernard Shaw, Mr.
George Moore, or even Mr. Oscar Wilde. They
never keep their head for very long out of the flood
of opinion. Mr. Bernard Shaw, the one brilliant
writer of comedy in England to-day, makes these
comedies something less than life by never forgetting
that he is a reformer, and Mr. Wilde could hardly
finish an act of a play without denouncing the British
public ; and Mr. Moore—God bless the hearers !—
has not for ten years now been able to keep himself
from the praise or blame of the Church of his fathers.
Goethe, whose mind was more busy with philosophy
than any modern poet, has said, 'The poet needs all
philosophy, but he must keep it out of his work.'
One remembers Dante, and wishes that Goethe had
left some commentary upon that saying, some defini-
tion of philosophy perhaps, but one cannot be less than
certain that the poet, though it may be well for him
to have right opinions, above all if his country be at
death's door, must keep all opinion that he holds to
merely because he thinks it right, out of his poetry,
if it is to be poetry at all. At the enquiry which pre-
ceded the granting of a patent to the Abbey Theatre
I was asked if *Cathleen ni Houlihan* was not written
to affect opinion. Certainly it was not. I had a
dream one night which gave me a story, and I had

certain emotions about this country, and I gave those
emotions expression for my own pleasure. If I had
written to convince others I would have asked my-
self, not 'Is that exactly what I think and feel?' but
'How would that strike so-and-so? How will they
think and feel when they have read it?' And all
would be oratorical and insincere. We only under-
stand our own minds, and the things that are striving
to utter themselves through our minds, and we move
others, not because we have understood or thought
about them at all, but because all life has the same
root. Coventry Patmore has said, 'The end of art
is peace,' and the following of art is little different
from the following of religion in the intense pre-
occupation that it demands. Somebody has said,
'God asks nothing of the highest soul except atten-
tion'; and so necessary is attention to mastery in any
art, that there are moments when one thinks that
nothing else is necessary, and nothing else so difficult.
The religious life has created for itself monasteries
and convents where men and women may forget in
prayer and contemplation everything that seems
necessary to the most useful and busy citizens of
their towns and villages, and one imagines that even
in the monastery and the convent there are passing
things, the twitter of a sparrow in the window, the
memory of some old quarrel, things lighter than air,
that keep the soul from its joy. How many of those
old religious sayings can one not apply to the life of
art? 'The Holy Spirit,' wrote S. Thomas A'Kempis,
'has liberated me from a multitude of opinions.'
When one sets out to cast into some mould so much
of life merely for life's sake, one is tempted at every

moment to twist it from its eternal shape to help some friend or harm some enemy. Alas, all men, we in Ireland more than others, are fighters, and it is a hard law that compels us to cast away our swords when we enter the house of the Muses, as men cast them away at the doors of the banqueting-hall at Tara. A weekly paper in reviewing last year's *Sambain*, convinced itself, or at any rate its readers—for that is the heart of the business in propaganda—that I only began to say these things a few months ago under I know not what alien influence; and yet I seem to have been saying them all my life. I took up an anthology of Irish verse that I edited some ten years ago, and I found them there, and I think they were a chief part of an old fight over the policy of the *New Irish Library*. Till they are accepted by writers and readers in this country it will never have a literature, it will never escape from the election rhyme and the pamphlet. So long as I have any control over the National Theatre Society it will be carried on in this spirit, call it art for art's sake if you will; and no plays will be produced at it which were written, not for the sake of a good story or fine verses or some revelation of character, but to please those friends of ours who are ever urging us to attack the priests or the English, or wanting us to put our imagination into handcuffs that we may be sure of never seeming to do one or the other.

I have had very little to say this year in *Sambain*, and I have said it badly. When I wrote *Ideas of Good and Evil* and *Celtic Twilight*, I wrote everything very slowly and a great many times over. A few years ago, however, my eyesight got so bad that I had to dictate the first drafts of everything, and then rewrite these drafts several times. I did the last *Samhain* this way, dictating all the thoughts in a few days, and rewriting them in two or three weeks ; but this time I am letting the first draft remain with all its carelessness of phrase and rhythm. I am busy with a practical project which needs the saying of many things from time to time, and it is better to say them carelessly and harshly than to take time from my poetry. One casts something away every year, and I shall, I think, have to cast away the hope of ever having a prose style that amounts to anything. After all, dictation gives one a certain vitality as of vehement speech.

1906

LITERATURE AND THE LIVING VOICE.*

I

ONE Sunday, in summer, a few years ago, I went to
the little village of Killeenan, that is not many miles
from Galway, to do honour to the memory of Raftery,
a Gaelic poet who died a little before the famine. A
headstone had been put over his grave in the half-
ruined churchyard, and a priest had come to bless it,
and many country people to listen to his poems.
After the shawled and frieze-coated people had knelt
down and prayed for the repose of his soul, they
gathered about a little wooden platform that had
been put up in a field. I do not remember whether
Raftery's poem about himself was one of those they
listened to, but certainly it was in the thoughts of
many, and it was the image reflected in that poem
that had drawn some of them from distant villages.

> I am Raftery the poet,
> Full of hope and love;
> With eyes without light;
> With gentleness without misery.
>
> Going west on my journey
> With the light of my heart;

* This essay was written immediately after the opening of the Abbey Theatre,
though it was not printed, through an accident, until the art of the Abbey has
become an art of peasant comedy. It tells of things we have never had the time
to begin. We still dream of them.—W.B.Y., *March*, 1908.

Weak and tired
To the end of my road.

I am now
And my back to a wall,
Playing music
To empty pockets.

Some few there remembered him, and one old
man came out among the reciters to tell of the
burying, where he himself, a young boy at the time,
had carried a candle.

The verses of other Gaelic poets were sung or
recited too, and, although certainly not often fine
poetry, they had its spirit, its *naïveté*—that is to say,
its way of looking at the world as if it were but an
hour old—its seriousness even in laughter, its per-
sonal rhythm.

A few days after I was in the town of Galway, and
saw there, as I had often seen in other country towns,
some young men marching down the middle of a
street singing an already outworn London music-hall
song, that filled the memory, long after they had
gone by, with a rhythm as pronounced and as im-
personal as the noise of a machine.   In the shop
windows there were, I knew, the signs of a life very
unlike that I had seen at Killeenan ; halfpenny comic
papers and story papers, sixpenny reprints of popular
novels, and, with the exception of a dusty Dumas or
Scott strayed thither, one knew not how, and one or
two little books of Irish ballads, nothing that one
calls literature, nothing that would interest the few
thousands who alone out of many millions have
what we call culture.   A few miles had divided the

sixteenth century, with its equality of culture, of good taste, from the twentieth, where if a man has fine taste he has either been born to leisure and opportunity or has in him an energy that is genius. One saw the difference in the clothes of the people of the town and of the village, for, as the Emerald tablet says, outward and inner things answer to one another. The village men wore their bawneens, their white flannel jackets ; they had clothes that had a little memory of clothes that had once been adapted to their calling by centuries of continual slight changes. They were sometimes well dressed, for they suggested nothing but themselves and wore little that had suited another better. But in the town nobody was well dressed ; for in modern life, only a few people—some few thousands—set the fashion, and set it to please themselves and to fit their lives, and as for the rest they must go shabby— the ploughman in clothes cut for a life of leisure, but made of shoddy, and the tramp in the ploughman's cast-off clothes, and the scarecrow in the tramp's battered coat and broken hat.

II

All that love the arts or love dignity in life have at one time or another noticed these things, and some have wondered why the world has for some three or four centuries sacrificed so much, and with what seems a growing recklessness, to create an intellectual aristocracy, a leisured class—to set apart, and above all others, a number of men and women who are not very well pleased with one another or the world they

have to live in. It is some comparison, like this
that I have made, which has been the origin, as I
think, of most attempts to revive some old language
in which the general business of the world is no
longer transacted. The Provençal movement, the
Welsh, the Czech, have all, I think, been attempt-
ing, when we examine them to the heart, to restore
what is called a more picturesque way of life, that
is to say, a way of life in which the common man
has some share in imaginative art. That this is the
decisive element in the attempt to revive and to
preserve the Irish language I am very certain. A
language enthusiast does not put it that way to
himself; he says, rather, 'If I can make the people
talk Irish again they will be the less English'; but
if you talk to him till you have hunted the words
into their burrow you will find that the word 'Ireland'
means to him a form of life delightful to his imagin-
ation, and that the word 'England' suggests to him
a cold, joyless, irreligious and ugly life. The life of
the villages, with its songs, its dances and its pious
greetings, its conversations full of vivid images
shaped hardly more by life itself than by innumerable
forgotten poets, all that life of good nature and
improvisation grows more noble as he meditates
upon it, for it mingles with the middle ages until he
no longer can see it as it is but as it was, when it
ran, as it were, into a point of fire in the courtliness
of kings' houses. He hardly knows whether what
stirred him yesterday was that old fiddler, playing
an almost-forgotten music on a fiddle mended with
twine, or a sudden thought of some king that was
of the blood of that old man, some O'Loughlin or

P

O'Byrne, listening amid his soldiers, he and they at the one table, they too, lucky, bright-eyed, while the minstrel sang of angry Cuchulain, or of him men called 'Golden salmon of the sea, clean hawk of the air.' It will not please him, however, if you tell him that he is fighting the modern world, which he calls 'England,' as Mistral and his fellows called it Paris, and that he will need more than language if he is to make the monster turn up its white belly. And yet the difference between what the word England means and all that the word Gaelic suggests is greater than any that could have been before the imagination of Mistral. Ireland, her imagination at its noon before the birth of Chaucer, has created the most beautiful literature of a whole people that has been anywhere since Greece and Rome, while English literature, the greatest of all literatures but that of Greece, is yet the literature of a few. Nothing of it but a handful of ballads about Robin Hood has come from the folk or belongs to them rightly, for the good English writers, with a few exceptions that seem accidental, have written for a small cultivated class ; and is not this the reason ? Irish poetry and Irish stories were made to be spoken or sung, while English literature, alone of great literatures, because the newest of them all, has all but completely shaped itself in the printing-press. In Ireland to-day the old world that sang and listened is, it may be for the last time in Europe, face to face with the world that reads and writes, and their antagonism is always present under some name or other in Irish imagination and intellect. I myself cannot be convinced that the printing-press will be always victor, for change is inconceivably

swift, and when it begins—well, as the proverb has
it, everything comes in at the hole. The world soon
tires of its toys, and our exaggerated love of print
and paper seems to me to come out of passing
conditions and to be no more a part of the final
constitution of things than the craving of a woman
in child-bed for green apples. When one takes a
book into the corner, one surrenders so much life
for one's knowledge, so much, I mean, of that
normal activity that gives one life and strength, one
lays away one's own handiwork and turns from one's
friend, and if the book is good one is at some pains
to press all the little wanderings and tumults of the
mind into silence and quiet. If the reader be poor,
if he has worked all day at the plough or the desk,
he will hardly have strength enough for any but a
meretricious book; nor is it only when the book is
on the knees that one's life must be given for it.
For a good and sincere book needs the preparation
of the peculiar studies and reveries that prepare for
good taste, and make it easier for the mind to find
pleasure in a new landscape; and all these reveries
and studies have need of so much time and thought
that it is almost certain a man cannot be a successful
doctor, or engineer, or Cabinet Minister, and have a
culture good enough to escape the mockery of the
ragged art student who comes of an evening some-
times to borrow a half-sovereign. The old culture
came to a man at his work; it was not at the expense
of life, but an exaltation of life itself; it came in at
the eyes as some civic ceremony sailed along the
streets, or as one arrayed oneself before the looking-
glass, or it came in at the ears in a song as one bent

over the plough or the anvil, or at that great table where rich and poor sat down together and heard the minstrel bidding them pass around the wine-cup and say a prayer for Gawain dead. Certainly it came without a price; it did not take one from one's friends and one's handiwork; but it was like a good woman who gives all for love and is never jealous and is ready to do all the talking when we are tired.

How the old is to come again, how the other side of the penny is to come up, how the spit is to turn the other side of the meat to the fire, I do not know, but that the time will come I am certain; when one kind of desire has been satisfied for a long time it becomes sleepy, and other kinds, long quiet, after making a noise begin to order life. Of the many things, desires or powers or instruments, that are to change the world, the artist is fitted to understand but two or three, and the less he troubles himself about the complexity that is outside his craft, the more will he find it all within his craft, and the more dexterous will his hand and his thought become. I am trying to see nothing in the world but the arts, and nothing in this change—which one cannot prove but only foretell—but the share my own art will have in it.

III

One thing is entirely certain. Wherever the old imaginative life lingers it must be stirred into life, and kept alive, and in Ireland this is the work, it may be, of the Gaelic movement. But the nineteenth century, with its moral zeal, its insistence upon irrelevant interests, having passed over, the artist can admit that he cares about nothing that does not give him a new subject or a new technique. Propaganda would be for him a dissipation, but he may compare his art, if he has a mind to, with the arts that belonged to a whole people, and discover, not how to imitate the external form of an epic or a folk-song, but how to express in some equivalent form whatever in the thoughts of his own age seem, as it were, to press into the future. The most obvious difference is that when literature belonged to a whole people, its three great forms, narrative, lyrical and dramatic, found their way to men's minds without the mediation of print and paper. That narrative poetry may find its minstrels again, and lyrical poetry adequate singers, and dramatic poetry adequate players, he must spend much of his time with these three lost arts, and the more technical is his interest the better. When I first began working in Ireland at what some newspaper has called the Celtic Renaissance, I saw that we had still even in English a sufficient audience for song and speech. Certain of our young men and women, too restless and sociable to be readers, had amongst them an interest in Irish legend and history, and years of imaginative politics had kept them from forgetting, as most modern people have, how to listen to serious words. I always saw that some kind of theatre would be a natural centre for a tradition of feeling and thought, but that it must—and this was its chief opportunity—appeal to the interest appealed to by lively conversation or by oratory. In other words, that it must be made for young people who were sufficiently ignorant to refuse a pound of flesh even though the Nine Worthies offered their wisdom in return. They are not, perhaps, very numerous, for they do not include the thousands of conquered spirits who in Dublin, as elsewhere, go to see *The Girl from Kay's*, or when Mr. Tree is upon tour, *The Girl from Prospero's Island*; and the peasant in Ireland, as elsewhere, has not taken to the theatre, and can, I think, be moved through Gaelic only.

If one could get them, I thought, one could draw to oneself the apathetic people who are in every country, and people who don't know what they like till somebody tells them. Now, a friend has given me that theatre. It is not very big, but it is quite big enough to seat those few thousands and their friends in a seven days' run of a new play; and I have begun my real business. I have to find once again singers, minstrels, and players who love words more than any other thing under heaven, for without fine words there is no literature.

IV

I will say but a little of dramatic technique, as I would have it in this theatre of speech, of romance, of extravagance, for I have written of all that so many times. In every art, when it seems to one that it has need of a renewing of life, one goes backwards till one lights upon a time when it was nearer to human life and instinct, before it had gathered about it so many mechanical specialisations and traditions. One examines that earlier condition and thinks out its principles of life, and one may be able to separate accidental from vital things. William Morris, for instance, studied the earliest printing, the founts of type that were made when men saw their craft with eyes that were still new, and with leisure, and without the restraints of commerce and custom. And then he made a type that was really new, that had the quality of his own mind about it, though it reminds one of its ancestry, of its high breeding as it were. Coleridge and Wordsworth were influenced by the publication of Percy's *Reliques* to the making of a simplicity altogether unlike that of old ballad-writers. Rossetti went to early Italian painting, to Holy Families and choirs of angels, that he might learn how to express an emotion that had its roots in sexual desire and in the delight of his generation in fine clothes and in beautiful rooms. Nor is it otherwise with the reformers of churches and of the social order, for reform must justify itself by a return in feeling to something that our fathers have told us in the old time.

So it is with us. Inspired by players who played before a figured curtain, we have made scenery, indeed, but scenery that is little more than a suggestion—a pattern with recurring boughs and leaves of gold for a wood, a great green curtain with a red stencil upon it to carry the eye upward for a palace, and so on. More important than these, we have looked for the centre of our art where the players of the time of Shakespeare and of Corneille found theirs, in speech, whether it be the perfect mimicry of the conversation of two countrymen of the roads, or that idealised speech poets have imagined for what we think but do not say. Before men read, the ear and the tongue were subtle, and delighted one another with the little tunes that were in words; every word would have its own tune, though but one main note may have been marked enough for us to name it. They loved language, and all literature was then, whether in the mouth of minstrels, players, or singers, but the perfection of an art that everybody practised, a flower out of the stem of life. And language continually renewed itself in that perfection, returning to daily life out of that finer leisure, strengthened and sweetened as from a retreat ordered by religion. The ordinary dramatic critic, when you tell him that a play, if it is to be of a great kind, must have beautiful words, will answer that you have misunderstood the nature of the stage and are asking of it what books should give. Sometimes when some excellent man, a playgoer certainly and sometimes a critic, has read me a passage out of some poet, I have been set wondering what books of poetry can mean to the greater number of men. If they are to read poetry at all, if they are to enjoy beautiful rhythm, if they are to get from poetry anything but what it has in common with prose, they must hear it spoken by men who have music in their voices and a learned understanding of its sound. There is no poem so great that a fine speaker cannot make it greater or that a bad ear cannot make it nothing. All the arts when young and happy are but the point of the spear whose handle is our daily life. When they grow old and unhappy they perfect themselves away from life, and life, seeing that they are sufficient to themselves, forgets them. The fruit of the tree that was in Eden grows out of a flower full of scent, rounds and ripens, until at last the little stem, that brought to it the sap out of the tree, dries up and breaks, and the fruit rots upon the ground.

The theatre grows more elaborate, developing the player at the expense of the poet, developing the scenery at the expense of the player, always increasing in importance whatever has come to it out of the mere mechanism of a building or the interests of a class, specialising more and more, doing whatever is easiest rather than what is most noble, and creating a class before the footlights as behind, who are stirred to excitements that belong to it and not to life; until at last life, which knows that a specialised energy is not herself, turns to other things, content to leave it to weaklings and triflers, to those in whose body there is the least quantity of herself.

V

But if we are to delight our three or four thousand young men and women with a delight that will follow them into their own houses, and if we are to add the countryman to their number, we shall need more than the play, we shall need those other spoken arts. The player rose into importance in the town, but the minstrel is of the country. We must have narrative as well as dramatic poetry, and we are making room for it in the theatre in the first instance, but in this also we must go to an earlier time. Modern recitation is not, like modern theatrical art, an over-elaboration of a true art, but an entire misunderstanding. It has no tradition at all. It is an endeavour to do what can only be done well by the player. It has no relation of its own to life. Some young man in evening clothes will recite to you *The Dream of Eugene Aram*, and it will be laughable, grotesque and a little vulgar. Tragic emotions that need scenic illusion, a long preparation, a gradual heightening of emotion, are thrust into the middle of our common affairs. That they may be as extravagant, as little tempered by anything ideal or distant as possible, he will break up the rhythm, regarding neither the length of the lines nor the natural music of the phrases, and distort the accent by every casual impulse. He will gesticulate wildly, adapting his movements to the drama as if Eugene Aram were in the room before us, and all the time we see a young man in evening dress who has become unaccountably insane. Nothing that he can do or say will make us forget that he is Mr. Robinson the bank clerk, and that the toes of his boots turn upward. We have nothing to learn here. We must go to the villages or we must go back hundreds of years to Wolfram of Eisenbach and the castles of Thuringia. In this, as in all other arts, one finds its law and its true purpose when one is near the source. The minstrel never dramatised anybody but himself. It was impossible, from the nature of the words the poet had put into his mouth, or that he had made for himself, that he should speak as another person. He will go no nearer to drama than we do in daily speech, and he will not allow you for any long time to forget himself. Our own Raftery will stop the tale to cry, 'This is what I, Raftery, wrote down in the book of the people'; or 'I, myself, Raftery, went to bed without supper that night.' Or, if it is Wolfram, and the tale is of Gawain or Parsival, he will tell the listening ladies that he sings of happy love out of his own unhappy love, or he will interrupt

the story of a siege and its hardships to remember
his own house, where there is not enough food for
the mice. He knows how to keep himself interesting
that his words may have weight—so many lines of
narrative, and then a phrase about himself and his
emotions. The reciter cannot be a player, for that is
a different art ; but he must be a messenger, and he
should be as interesting, as exciting, as are all that
carry great news. He comes from far off, and he
speaks of far-off things with his own peculiar
animation, and instead of lessening the ideal and
beautiful elements of speech, he may, if he has a
mind to, increase them. He may speak to actual
notes as a singer does if they are so simple that he
never loses the speaking-voice, and if the poem is
long he must do so, or his own voice will become
weary and formless. His art is nearer to pattern
than that of the player. It is always allusion, never
illusion ; for what he tells of, no matter how im-
passioned he may become, is always distant, and for
this reason he may permit himself every kind of
nobleness. In a short poem he may interrupt the
narrative with a burden, which the audience will soon
learn to sing, and this burden, because it is repeated
and need not tell a story to a first hearing, can have
a more elaborate musical notation, can go nearer to
ordinary song. Gradually other devices will occur
to him—effects of loudness and softness, of increasing
and decreasing speed, certain rhythmic movements
of his body, a score of forgotten things, for the art
of speech is lost, and when one begins at it every day
is a discovery. The reciter must be made exciting
and wonderful in himself, apart from what he has to

tell, and that is more difficult than it was in the middle ages. We are not mysterious to one another ; we can come from far off and yet be no better than our neighbours. We are no longer like those Egyptian birds that flew out of Arabia, their claws full of spices ; nor can we, like an ancient or mediæval poet, throw into our verses the emotions and events of our lives, or even dramatise, as they could, the life of the minstrel into whose mouth we are to put our words. I can think of nothing better than to borrow from the tellers of old tales, who will often pretend to have been at the wedding of the princess or afterwards 'when they were throwing out children by the basketful,' and to give the story-teller definite fictitious personality and find for him an appropriate costume. Many costumes and persons come into my imagination. I imagine an old countryman upon the stage of the theatre or in some little country court-house where a Gaelic society is meeting, and I can hear him say that he is Raftery or a brother, and that he has tramped through France and Spain and the whole world. He has seen everything, and he has all country love tales at his finger-tips. I can imagine, too—and now the story-teller is more serious and more naked of country circumstance—a jester with black cockscomb and black clothes. He has been in the faery hills ; perhaps he is the terrible *Amadan-na-Breena* himself ; or he has been so long in the world that he can tell of ancient battles. It is not as good as what we have lost, but we cannot hope to see in our time, except by some rare accident, the minstrel who differs from his audience in nothing but the exaltation of his mood, and who is yet as exciting and as romantic in their eyes as were Raftery and Wolfram to their people.

It is perhaps nearly impossible to make recitation a living thing, for there is no existing taste one can appeal to ; but it should not be hard here in Ireland to interest people in songs that are made for the word's sake and not for the music, or for that only in a secondary degree. They are interested in such songs already, only the songs have little subtilty of thought and of language. One does not find in them that modern emotion which seems new because it has been brought so very lately out of the cellar. At their best they are the songs of children and of country people, eternally young for all their centuries, and yet not even in old days, as one thinks, the art of kings' houses. We require a method of setting to music that will make it possible to sing or to speak to notes a poem like Rossetti's translation of *The Ballad of Dead Ladies* in such a fashion that no word shall have an intonation or accentuation it could not have in passionate speech. It must be set for the speaking-voice, like the songs that sailors make up or remember, and a man at the far end of the room must be able to take it down on a first hearing. An English musical paper said the other day, in commenting on something I had written, ' Owing to musical necessities, vowels must be lengthened in singing to an extent which in speech would be ludicrous if not absolutely impossible.' I have but one art, that of speech, and my feeling for music dissociated from speech is very slight, and listening as I do to the words with the better part of my attention, there is no modern song sung in the modern way that is not to my taste 'ludicrous' and 'impossible.' I hear with older ears than the musician, and the songs of country people and of sailors delight me. I wonder why the musician is not content to set to music some arrangement of meaningless liquid vowels, and thereby to make his song like that of the birds ; but I do not judge his art for any purpose but my own.* It is worthless for my purpose certainly, and it is one of the causes that are bringing about in modern countries a degradation of language. I have to find men with more music than I have, who will develop to a finer subtilty the singing of the cottage and the forecastle, and develop it more on the side of speech than that of music, until it has become intellectual and nervous enough to be the vehicle of a Shelley or a Keats. For some purposes it will be necessary to divine the lineaments of a still older art, and re-create the regulated declamations that died out when music fell into its earliest elaborations. Miss Farr has divined enough of this older art, of which no fragment has come down to us—for even the music of *Aucassin and Nicolette*, with its definite tune, its recurring pattern of sound, is something more than declamation—to make the chorus of *Hippolytus* and of the *Trojan Women*, at the Court Theatre or the Lyric, intelligible speech, even when several voices spoke together. She used very often definite melodies of a very simple kind, but always when the thought became intricate and the

---

* I have heard musicians excuse themselves by claiming that they put the words there for the sake of the singer ; but if that be so, why should not the singer sing something she may wish to have by rote ? Nobody will hear the words ; and the local time-table, or, so much suet and so many raisins, and so much spice and so much sugar, and whether it is to be put in a quick or a slow oven, would run very nicely with a little management.

measure grave and slow, fell back upon declamation
regulated by notes. Her experiments have included
almost every kind of verse, and every possible
elaboration of sound compatible with the supremacy
of the words. I do not think Homer is ever so
moving as when she recites him to a little tune played
on a stringed instrument not very unlike a lyre.
She began at my suggestion with songs in plays, for
it was clearly an absurd thing that words necessary
to one's understanding of the action, either because
they explained some character, or because they carried
some emotion to its highest intensity, should be less
intelligible than the bustling and ruder words of the
dialogue. We have tried our art, since we first tried
it in a theatre, upon many kinds of audiences, and
have found that ordinary men and women take
pleasure in it and sometimes tell one that they never
understood poetry before. It is, however, more
difficult to move those, fortunately for our purpose
but a few, whose ears are accustomed to the abstract
emotion and elaboration of notes in modern music.

VI

If we accomplish this great work, if we make it
possible again for the poet to express himself, not
merely through words, but through the voices of
singers, of minstrels, of players, we shall certainly
have changed the substance and the manner of our
poetry. Everyone who has to interest his audience
through the voice discovers that his success depends
upon the clear, simple and varied structure of his
thought. I have written a good many plays in verse

and prose, and almost all those plays I have re-written after performance, sometimes again and again, and every change that has succeeded has been an addition to the masculine element, an increase of strength in the bony structure.

Modern literature, above all poetical literature, is monotonous in its structure and effeminate in its continual insistence upon certain moments of strained lyricism. William Morris, who did more than any modern to recover mediæval art, did not in his *Earthly Paradise* copy from Chaucer, from whom he copied so much that was *naïve* and beautiful, what seems to me essential in Chaucer's art. He thought of himself as writing for the reader, who could return to him again and again when the chosen mood had come, and became monotonous, melancholy, too continuously lyrical in his understanding of emotion and of life. Had he accustomed himself to read out his poems upon those Sunday evenings that he gave to Socialist speeches, and to gather an audience of average men, precisely such an audience as I have often seen in his house, he would have been forced to Chaucer's variety, to his delight in the height and depth, and would have found expression for that humorous many-sided nature of his. I owe to him many truths, but I would add to those truths the certainty that all the old writers, the masculine writers of the world, wrote to be spoken or to be sung, and in a later age to be read aloud, for hearers who had to understand swiftly or not at all, and who gave up nothing of life to listen, but sat, the day's work over, friend by friend, lover by lover.

THE ARROW: 1906.*

THE SEASON'S WORK.

A character of the winter's work will be the large number of romantic, poetic and historical plays—that is to say, of plays which require a convention for their performance; their speech, whether it be verse or prose, being so heightened as to transcend that of any form of real life. Our first two years of The Abbey Theatre have been expended mostly on the perfecting of the Company in peasant comedy and tragedy. Every national dramatic movement or theatre in countries like Bohemia and Hungary, as in Elizabethan England, has arisen out of a study of the common people, who preserve national characteristics more than any other class, and out of an imaginative recreation of national history or legend. The life of the drawing-room, the life represented in most plays of the ordinary theatre of to-day, differs but little all over the world, and has as little to do with the national spirit as the architecture of, let us say, St. Stephen's Green, or Queen's Gate, or of the Boulevards about the Arc de Triomphe.

As we wish our work to be full of the life of this country, our stage-manager has almost always to train our actors from the beginning, always so in the case of peasant plays, and this makes the building up of a theatre like ours the work of years. We are now fairly satisfied with the representation of peasant life, and we can afford to give the greater part of our attention to other expressions of our art and of our life. The romantic work and poetical work once

* *The Arrow*, a briefer chronicle than *Samhain*, was distributed with the programme for a few months.

Q

reasonably good, we can, if but the dramatist arrive,
take up the life of our drawing-rooms, and see if
there is something characteristic there, something
which our nationality may enable us to express better
than others, and so create plays of that life and means
to play them as truthful as a play of Hauptmann's
or of Ibsen's upon the German or Scandinavian stage.
I am not myself interested in this kind of work, and
do not believe it to be as important as contemporary
critics think it is, but a theatre such as we project
· should give a reasonably complete expression to the
imaginative interests of its country. In any case it
was easier, and therefore wiser, to begin where our
art is most unlike that of others, with the represen-
tation of country life.

It is possible to speak the universal truths of
human nature whether the speakers be peasants or
wealthy men, for—

> 'Love doth sing
> As sweetly in a beggar as a king.'

So far as we have any model before us it is the
national and municipal theatre in various Continental
towns, and, like the best of these, we must have in
our repertory masterpieces from every great school
of dramatic literature, and play them confidently,
even though the public be slow to like that old stern
art, and perhaps a little proudly, remembering that
no other English-speaking theatre can be so catholic.
Certainly the weathercocks of our imagination will
not turn those painted eyes of theirs too long to the
quarter of the Scandinavian winds. If the wind blow
long from the Mediterranean, the paint may peel
before we pray for a change in the weather.

THE CONTROVERSY OVER
THE PLAYBOY OF THE WESTERN WORLD.

We have claimed for our writers the freedom to find in their own land every expression of good and evil necessary to their art, for Irish life contains, like all vigorous life, the seeds of all good and evil, and a writer must be free here as elsewhere to watch where weed or flower ripen. No one who knows the work of our Theatre as a whole can say we have neglected the flower; but the moment a writer is forbidden to take pleasure in the weed, his art loses energy and abundance. In the great days of English dramatic art the greatest English writer of comedy was free to create *The Alchemist* and *Volpone,* but a demand born of Puritan conviction and shop-keeping timidity and insincerity, for what many second-rate intellects thought to be noble and elevating events and characters, had already at the outset of the eighteenth century ended the English drama as a complete and serious art. Sheridan and Goldsmith, when they restored comedy after an epoch of sentimentalities, had to apologise for their satiric genius by scenes of conventional love-making and sentimental domesticity that have set them outside the company of all, whether their genius be great or little, whose work is pure and whole. The quarrel of our Theatre to-day is the quarrel of the Theatre in many lands; for the old Puritanism, the old dislike of power and reality have not changed, even when they are called by some Gaelic name.

[On the second performance of *The Playboy of the Western World* about forty men who sat in the middle of the pit succeeded in making the play entirely inaudible. Some of them brought tin-trumpets, and the noise began immediately on the rise of the curtain. For days articles in the Press called for the withdrawal of the play, but we played for the seven nights we had announced; and before the week's end opinion had turned in our favour. There were, however, nightly disturbances and a good deal of rioting in the surrounding streets. On the last night of the play there were, I believe, five hundred police keeping order in the theatre and in its neighbourhood. Some days later our enemies, though beaten so far as the play was concerned, crowded into the cheaper seats for a debate on the freedom of the stage. They were very excited, and kept up the discussion until near twelve. The last paragraphs of my opening statement ran as follows.]

From Mr. Yeats' opening Speech in the Debate on February 4, 1907, at the Abbey Theatre.

The struggle of the last week has been long a necessity; various paragraphs in newspapers describing Irish attacks on Theatres had made many worthy young men come to think that the silencing of a stage at their own pleasure, even if hundreds desired that it should not be silenced, might win them a little fame, and, perhaps, serve their country. Some of these attacks have been made on plays which are in themselves indefensible, vulgar and old-fashioned farces and comedies. But the attack, being an annihilation of civil rights, was never anything but an increase of Irish disorder. The last I heard of was in Liverpool, and there a stage was rushed, and a priest, who had set a play upon it, withdrew his play and apologised to the audience. We have not such pliant bones, and did not learn in the houses that bred us a so suppliant knee. But behind the excitement of example there is a more fundamental movement of opinion. Some seven or eight years ago the National movement was democratised and passed from the hands of a few leaders into those of large numbers of young men organised in clubs and societies. These young men made the mistake of the newly-enfranchised everywhere ; they fought for causes worthy in themselves with the unworthy instruments of tyranny and violence. Comic songs of a certain kind were to be driven from the stage, everyone was to wear Irish cloth, everyone was to learn Irish, everyone was to hold certain opinions, and these ends were sought by personal attacks, by virulent caricature and violent derision. It needs eloquence to persuade and knowledge to expound ; but the coarser means come ready to every man's hand, as ready as a stone or a stick, and where these coarse means are all, there is nothing but mob, and the commonest idea most prospers and is most sought for.

Gentlemen of the little clubs and societies, do not mistake the meaning of our victory; it means something for us, but more for you. When the curtain of *The Playboy* fell on Saturday night in the midst of what *The Sunday Independent*—no friendly witness— described as 'thunders of applause,' I am confident that I saw the rise in this country of a new thought, a new opinion, that we had long needed. It was not all approval of Mr. Synge's play that sent the receipts of the Abbey Theatre this last week to twice the height they had ever touched before. The generation of young men and girls who are now leaving schools or colleges are weary of the tyranny of clubs and leagues. They wish again for individual sincerity, the eternal quest of truth, all that has been given up for so long that all might crouch upon the one roost and quack or cry in the one flock. We are beginning once again to ask what a man is, and to be content to wait a little before we go on to that further question : What is a good Irishman ? There are some who have not yet their degrees that will say to friend or neighbour, 'You have voted with the English, and that is bad'; or 'You have sent away your Irish servants, or thrown away your Irish clothes, or blacked your face for your singing. I despise what you have done, I keep you still my friend; but if you are terrorised out of doing any of these things, evil things though I know them to be, I will not have you for my friend any more.' Manhood is all, and the root of manhood is courage and courtesy.

1907

ON TAKING *THE PLAYBOY* TO LONDON.

The failure of the audience to understand this powerful and strange work (*The Playboy of the Western World*) has been the one serious failure of our movement, and it could not have happened but that the greater number of those who came to shout down the play were no regular part of our audience at all, but members of parties and societies whose main interests are political. We have been denounced with even greater violence than on the first production of the play for announcing that we should carry it to London. We cannot see that an attack, which we believe to have been founded on a misunderstanding of the nature of literature, should prevent us from selecting, as our custom is, whatever of our best comes within the compass of our players at the time, to show in some English theatres. Nearly all strong and strange writing is attacked on its appearance, and those who press it upon the world may not cease from pressing it, for their justification is its ultimate acceptance. Ireland is passing through a crisis in the life of the mind greater than any she has known since the rise of the Young Ireland party, and based upon a principle which sets many in opposition to the habits of thought and feeling come down from that party, for the seasons change, and need and occupation with them. Many are beginning to recognise the right of the individual mind to see the world in its own way, to cherish the thoughts which separate

men from one another, and that are the creators of
distinguished life, instead of those thoughts that had
made one man like another if they could, and have
but succeeded in setting hysteria and insincerity in
place of confidence and self-possession. To the Young
Ireland writers, who have the ear of Ireland, though
not its distracted mind, truth was historical and ex-
ternal and not a self-consistent personal vision, and it
is but according to ancient custom that the new truth
should force its way amid riot and great anger.

APPENDIX I

THE HOUR-GLASS.

This play is founded upon the following story, recorded by Lady Wilde in *Ancient Legends of Ireland,* 1887, vol. i., pp. 60-67 :—

THE PRIEST'S SOUL.

In former days there were great schools in Ireland where every sort of learning was taught to the people, and even the poorest had more knowledge at that time than many a gentleman has now. But as to the priests, their learning was above all, so that the fame of Ireland went over the whole world, and many kings from foreign lands used to send their sons all the way to Ireland to be brought up in the Irish schools.

Now, at this time there was a little boy learning at one of them who was a wonder to every one for his cleverness. His parents were only labouring people, and of course very poor ; but young as he was, and poor as he was, no king's or lord's son could come up to him in learning. Even the masters were put to shame ; for when they were trying to teach him he would tell them something they had never heard of before, and show them their ignorance. One of his great triumphs was in argument, and he would go on till he proved to you that black was white, and then when you gave in, for no one could beat him in talk, he would turn round and show you that white was black, or may be that there was no colour at all in the world. When he grew up his poor father and mother were so proud of him that they resolved to make him a priest, which they did at last, though they nearly starved themselves to get the money. Well, such another learned man was not in Ireland, and he was as great in argument as ever, so that no one could stand

before him.   Even the Bishops tried to talk to him, but he
showed them at once they knew nothing at all.

Now, there were no schoolmasters in those times, but it
was the priests taught the people ; and as this man was the
cleverest in Ireland all the foreign kings sent their sons to
him as long as he had house-room to give them. So he grew
very proud, and began to forget how low he had been, and,
worst of all, even to forget God, who had made him what
he was.   And the pride of arguing got hold of him, so that
from one thing to another he went on to prove that there
was no Purgatory, and then no Hell, and then no Heaven,
and then no God ; and at last that men had no souls, but
were no more than a dog or a cow, and when they died
there was an end of them.   'Who ever saw a soul ?' he
would say.   'If you can show me one, I will believe.'   No
one could make any answer to this; and at last they all came
to believe that as there was no other world, every one might
do what they liked in this, the priest setting the example,
for he took a beautiful young girl to wife.   But as no priest
or bishop in the whole land could be got to marry them, he
was obliged to read the service over for himself.   It was a
great scandal, yet no one dared to say a word, for all the
kings' sons were on his side, and would have slaughtered any
one who tried to prevent his wicked goings-on.   Poor boys !
they all believed in him, and thought every word he said
was the truth.   In this way his notions began to spread
about, and the whole world was going to the bad, when one
night an angel came down from Heaven, and told the priest
he had but twenty-four hours to live.   He began to tremble,
and asked for a little more time.

But the angel was stiff, and told him that could not be.

'What do you want time for, you sinner ?' he asked.

'Oh, sir, have pity on my poor soul !' urged the priest.

'Oh, ho ! You have a soul, then ?' said the angel. 'Pray
how did you find that out ?'

'It has been fluttering in me ever since you appeared,'

answered the priest. 'What a fool I was not to think of it before!'

'A fool, indeed,' said the angel. 'What good was all your learning, when it could not tell you that you had a soul?'

'Ah, my lord,' said the priest, 'if I am to die, tell me how soon I may be in heaven.'

'Never,' replied the angel. 'You denied there was a Heaven.'

'Then, my lord, may I go to Purgatory?'

'You denied Purgatory also; you must go straight to Hell,' said the angel.

'But, my lord, I denied Hell also,' answered the priest, 'so you can't send me there either.'

The angel was a little puzzled.

'Well,' said he, 'I'll tell you what I can do for you. You may either live now on earth for a hundred years enjoying every pleasure, and then be cast into Hell for ever; or you may die in twenty-four hours in the most horrible torments, and pass through Purgatory, there to remain till the Day of Judgment, if only you can find some one person that believes, and through his belief mercy will be vouchsafed to you and your soul will be saved.'

The priest did not take five minutes to make up his mind.

'I will have death in the twenty-four hours,' he said, 'so that my soul may be saved at last.'

On this the angel gave him directions as to what he was to do, and left him.

Then, immediately, the priest entered the large room where all his scholars and the kings' sons were seated, and called out to them—

'Now, tell me the truth, and let none fear to contradict me. Tell me what is your belief. Have men souls?'

'Master,' they answered, 'once we believed that men had souls; but, thanks to your teaching, we believe so no longer. There is no Hell, and no Heaven, and no God. This is our belief, for it is thus you taught us.'

Then the priest grew pale with fear, and cried out: 'Listen! I taught you a lie. There is a God, and man has an immortal soul. I believe now all I denied before.'

But the shouts of laughter that rose up drowned the priest's voice, for they thought he was only trying them for argument.

'Prove it, master,' they cried, 'prove it! Who has ever seen God? Who has ever seen the soul?'

And the room was stirred with their laughter.

The priest stood up to answer them, but no word could he utter; all his eloquence, all his powers of argument, had gone from him, and he could do nothing but wring his hands and cry out—

'There is a God! there is a God! Lord, have mercy on my soul!'

And they all began to mock him, and repeat his own words that he had taught them—

'Show him to us; show us your God.'

And he fled from them groaning with agony, for he saw that none believed, and how then could his soul be saved?

But he thought next of his wife.

'She will believe,' he said to himself. 'Women never give up God.'

And he went to her; but she told him that she believed only what he taught her, and that a good wife should believe in her husband first, and before and above all things in heaven or earth.

Then despair came on him, and he rushed from the house and began to ask every one he met if they believed. But the same answer came from one and all: 'We believe only what you have taught us,' for his doctrines had spread far and wide through the county.

Then he grew half mad with fear, for the hours were passing. And he flung himself down on the ground in a lonesome spot, and wept and groaned in terror, for the time was coming fast when he must die.

Just then a little child came by.

'God save you kindly,' said the child to him.

The priest started up.

'Child, do you believe in God?' he asked.

'I have come from a far country to learn about Him,' said the child. 'Will your honour direct me to the best school that they have in these parts?'

'The best school and the best teacher is close by,' said the priest, and he named himself.

'Oh, not to that man,' answered the child, 'for I am told he denies God and Heaven and Hell, and even that man has a soul, because we can't see it; but I would soon put him down.'

The priest looked at him earnestly. 'How?' he inquired.

'Why,' said the child, 'I would ask him if he believed he had life to show me his life.'

'But he could not do that, my child,' said the priest. 'Life cannot be seen; we have it, but it is invisible.'

'Then, if we have life, though we cannot see it, we may also have a soul, though it is invisible,' answered the child.

When the priest heard him speak these words he fell down on his knees before him, weeping for joy, for now he knew his soul was safe; he had met at last one that believed. And he told the child his whole story: all his wickedness, and pride, and blasphemy against the great God; and how the angel had come to him and told him of the only way in which he could be saved, through the faith and prayers of some one that believed.

'Now, then,' he said to the child, 'take this penknife and strike it into my breast, and go on stabbing the flesh until you see the paleness of death on my face. Then watch— for a living thing will soar up from my body as I die, and you will then know that my soul has ascended to the presence of God. And when you see this thing, make haste and run to my school and call on all my scholars to come and see that the soul of their master has left the body, and that all he taught them was a lie, for that there is a God who punishes sin, and a Heaven and a Hell, and that man has an immortal soul, destined for eternal happiness or misery.'

'I will pray,' said the child, 'to have courage to do this work.'

And he kneeled down and prayed. Then when he rose up he took the penknife and struck it into the priest's heart, and struck and struck again till all the flesh was lacerated; but still the priest lived, though the agony was horrible, for he could not die until the twenty-four hours had expired. At last the agony seemed to cease, and the stillness of death settled on his face. Then the child, who was watching, saw a beautiful living creature, with four snow-white wings, mount from the dead man's body into the air and go fluttering round his head.

So he ran to bring the scholars; and when they saw it they all knew it was the soul of their master, and they watched with wonder and awe until it passed from sight into the clouds.

And this was the first butterfly that was ever seen in Ireland; and now all men know that the butterflies are the souls of the dead waiting for the moment when they may enter Purgatory, and so pass through torture to purification and peace.

But the schools of Ireland were quite deserted after that time, for people said, What is the use of going so far to learn when the wisest man in all Ireland did not know if he had a soul till he was near losing it; and was only saved at last through the simple belief of a little child?

The Hour-Glass was first played in The Molesworth Hall, Dublin, with the following cast:—Wise Man, Mr. T. Dudley Digges; His Wife, Miss M. T. Quinn; The Fool, Mr. F. J. Fay; Pupils, P. J. Kelly, P. Columb, C. Caufield.

We always play it in front of an olive-green curtain, and dress the Wise Man and his Pupils in various shades of

purple. Because in all these decorative schemes one needs,
as I think, a third colour subordinate to the other two, we
have partly dressed the Fool in red-brown, which is repeated
in the furniture. There is some green in his dress and in that
of the Wife of the Wise Man who is dressed mainly in
purple.

One sometimes has need of more lines of the little song,
and I have put into English rhyme three of the many verses
of a Gaelic ballad:

> I was going the road one day
> (O the brown and the yellow beer !)
> And I met with a man that was no right man
> (O my dear, my dear).
>
> 'Give me your wife,' said he,
> (O the brown and the yellow beer !)
> 'Till the sun goes down and an hour of the clock'
> (O my dear, my dear).
>
> 'Good-bye, good-bye, my husband,'
> (O the brown and the yellow beer !)
> 'For a year and a day by the clock of the sun'
> (O my dear, my dear).

APPENDIX II

CATHLEEN NI HOULIHAN.

My dear Lady Gregory,—

When I was a boy I used to wander about at Rosses Point and Ballisodare listening to old songs and stories. I wrote down what I heard and made poems out of the stories or put them into the little chapters of the first edition of *The Celtic Twilight*, and that is how I began to write in the Irish way.

Then I went to London to make my living, and though I spent a part of every year in Ireland and tried to keep the old life in my memory by reading every country tale I could find in books or old newspapers, I began to forget the true countenance of country life. The old tales were still alive for me indeed, but with a new, strange, half-unreal life, as if in a wizard's glass, until at last, when I had finished *The Secret Rose*, and was half-way through *The Wind Among the Reeds*, a wise woman in her trance told me that my inspiration was from the moon, and that I should always live close to water, for my work was getting too full of those little jewelled thoughts that come from the sun and have no nation. I had no need to turn to my books of astrology to know that the common people are under the moon, or to Porphyry to remember the image-making power of the waters. Nor did I doubt the entire truth of what she said to me, for my head was full of fables that I had no longer the knowledge and emotion to write. Then you brought me with you to see your friends in the cottages, and to talk to old wise men on Slieve Echtge, and we gathered together, or you gathered for me, a great number of stories and traditional beliefs. You taught me to understand again, and much more perfectly than before, the true countenance of country life.

One night I had a dream almost as distinct as a vision,
of a cottage where there was well-being and firelight and
talk of a marriage, and into the midst of that cottage there
came an old woman in a long cloak. She was Ireland her-
self, that Cathleen ni Houlihan for whom so many songs
have been sung and about whom so many stories have been
told and for whose sake so many have gone to their death.
I thought if I could write this out as a little play I could
make others see my dream as I had seen it, but I could
not get down out of that high window of dramatic verse,
and in spite of all you had done for me I had not the country
speech. One has to live among the people, like you, of
whom an old man said in my hearing, 'She has been a serv-
ing-maid among us,' before one can think the thoughts of
the people and speak with their tongue. We turned my
dream into the little play, *Cathleen ni Houlihan*, and when
we gave it to the little theatre in Dublin and found that the
working-people liked it, you helped me to put my other
dramatic fables into speech. Some of these have already been
acted, but some may not be acted for a long time, but all
seem to me, though they were but a part of a summer's
work, to have more of that countenance of country life than
anything I have done since I was a boy.

Feb., 1903.   W. B. YEATS.

This play was first played on April 2, 1902, in St.
Teresa's Hall, Dublin, with the following cast :—Cathleen,
Miss Maude Gonne; Delia Cahel, Miss Maire nic Sheublagh;
Bridget Gillan, Miss M. T. Quinn; Patrick Gillan, Mr. C.
Caufield; Michael Gillan, Mr. T. Dudley Digges; Peter
Gillan, Mr. W. G. Fay.

Miss Maude Gonne played very finely, and her great
height made Cathleen seem a divine being fallen into our
mortal infirmity. Since then the part has been twice played
in America by women who insisted on keeping their young
faces, and one of these when she came to the door dropped

R

her cloak, as I have been told, and showed a white satin dress embroidered with shamrocks. Upon another,—or was it the same occasion?—the player of Bridget wore a very becoming dress of the time of Louis the Fourteenth. The most beautiful woman of her time, when she played my Cathleen, 'made up' centuries old, and never should the part be played but with a like sincerity. This was the first play of our Irish School of folk-drama, and in it that way of quiet movement and careful speech which has given our players some little fame first showed itself, arising partly out of deliberate opinion and partly out of the ignorance of the players. Does art owe most to ignorance or to knowledge? Certainly it comes to its deathbed full of knowledge. I cannot imagine this play, or any folk-play of our school, acted by players with no knowledge of the peasant, and of the awkwardness and stillness of bodies that have followed the plough, or too lacking in humility to copy these things without convention or caricature.

The lines beginning 'Do not make a great keening' and 'They shall be remembered for ever' are said or sung to an air heard by one of the players in a dream. This music is with the other music at the end of the third volume.

APPENDIX III

THE GOLDEN HELMET.

The Golden Helmet was produced at the Abbey Theatre on March 19, 1908, with the following cast:—Cuchulain, J. M. Kerrigan; Conal, Arthur Sinclair; Leagerie, Fred. O' Donovan; Laeg, Sydney Morgan; Emer, Sara Allgood; Conal's Wife, Maire O'Neill; Leagerie's Wife, Eileen O' Doherty; Red Man, Ambrose Power; Horseboys, Scullions, and Black Men, S. Hamilton, T. J. Fox, U. Wright, D. Robertson, T. O'Neill, I. A. O'Rourke, P. Kearney.

In performance we left the black hands to the imagination, and probably when there is so much noise and movement on the stage they would always fail to produce any effect. Our stage is too small to try the experiment, for they would be hidden by the figures of the players. We staged the play with a very pronounced colour-scheme, and I have noticed that the more obviously decorative is the scene and costuming of any play, the more it is lifted out of time and place, and the nearer to faeryland do we carry it. One gets also much more effect out of concerted movements—above all, if there are many players—when all the clothes are the same colour. No breadth of treatment gives monotony when there is movement and change of lighting. It concentrates attention on every new effect and makes every change of outline or of light and shadow surprising and delightful. Because of this one can use contrasts of colour, between clothes and background, or in the background itself, the complementary colours for instance, which would be too obvious to keep the attention in a painting. One wishes to make the movement of the action as important as possible, and the simplicity which gives depth of colour does this, just as, for precisely similar reasons, the lack of colour in a statue fixes the attention upon the form.

The play is founded upon an old Irish story, *The Feast of Bricriu*, given in *Cuchulain of Muirthemne*, and is meant as an introduction to *On Baile's Strand*.

APPENDIX IV

DATES AND PLACES OF
THE FIRST PERFORMANCE OF NEW PLAYS
PRODUCED BY THE NATIONAL THEATRE
SOCIETY AND ITS PREDECESSORS:—

1899.

IRISH LITERARY THEATRE AT ANTIENT CONCERT ROOMS.

May 8th. *The Countess Cathleen*, by W. B. Yeats.

May 9th. *The Heather Field*, by Edward Martyn.

1900.

IRISH LITERARY THEATRE AT THE GAIETY THEATRE.

Feb. 19th. { *The Last Feast of the Fianna*, by Alice Milligan.
Maeve, by Edward Martyn.

Feb. 20th. *The Bending of the Bough*, by George Moore.

1901.

Oct. 21st. *Diarmuid and Grania*, by W. B. Yeats and George Moore.

The Twisting of the Rope, by Douglas Hyde (first Gaelic play produced in a theatre).

1902.

MR. W. G. FAY'S IRISH NATIONAL DRAMATIC COM-
PANY AT ST. TERESA'S HALL, CLARENDON STREET.

April 2nd. { *Deirdre*, by 'A.E.'
{ *Cathleen ni Houlihan*, by W. B. Yeats.

IRISH NATIONAL DRAMATIC COMPANY AT ANTIENT
CONCERT ROOMS.

Oct. 29th. { *The Sleep of the King*, by Seumas O'Cuisin.
{ *The Laying of the Foundations*, by Fred
{ Ryan.
Oct. 30th. *A Pot of Broth*, by W. B. Yeats.
Oct. 31st. *The Racing Lug*, by Seumas O'Cuisin.

1903.

IRISH NATIONAL THEATRE SOCIETY, MOLESWORTH
HALL.

March 14th.{ *The Hour-Glass*, by W. B. Yeats.
{ *Twenty-five*, by Lady Gregory.
Oct. 8th. { *The King's Threshold*, by W. B. Yeats.
{ *In the Shadow of the Glen*, by J. M. Synge.
Dec. 3rd. *Broken Soil*, by P. Colm.

1904.

Jan. 14th. { *The Shadowy Waters*, by W. B. Yeats.
{ *The Townland of Tamney*, by Seumas
{ MacManus.
Feb. 25th. *Riders to the Sea*, by J. M. Synge.

IRISH NATIONAL THEATRE SOCIETY AT THE ABBEY
THEATRE.

Dec. 27th. { *On Baile's Strand*, by W. B. Yeats.
{ *Spreading the News*, by Lady Gregory.

1905.

Feb. 4th.   *The Well of the Saints*, by J. M. Synge.
March 25th.   *Kincora*, by Lady Gregory.
April 25th.   *The Building Fund*, by William Boyle.
June 9th.   *The Land*, by P. Colm.

NATIONAL THEATRE SOCIETY, LTD.

Dec. 9th.   *The White Cockade*, by Lady Gregory.

1906.

Jan. 20th.   *The Eloquent Dempsey*, by William Boyle.
Feb. 19th.   *Hyacinth Halvey*, by Lady Gregory.
Oct. 20th.   { *The Gaol Gate*, by Lady Gregory.
              { *The Mineral Workers*, by William Boyle.
Nov. 24th.   *Deirdre*, by W. B. Yeats.
Dec. 8th.   { *The Shadowy Waters* (new version), by
              {   W. B. Yeats.
              { *The Canavans*, by Lady Gregory.

1907.

Jan. 26th.   *The Playboy of the Western World*, by J.
                 M. Synge.
Feb. 23rd.   *The Jackdaw*, by Lady Gregory.
March 9th.   *Rising of the Moon*, by Lady Gregory.
April 1st.   *The Eyes of the Blind*, by Miss W. M.
                 Letts.
April 3rd.   *The Poorhouse*, by Lady Gregory and
                 Douglas Hyde.
April 27th.   *Fand*, by Wilfred Scawen Blunt.
Oct. 3rd.   *The Country Dressmaker*, by George
                 Fitzmaurice.

Oct. 31st. {
Dervorgilla, by Lady Gregory.
The Canavans (new version), by Lady Gregory.
}

Nov. 21st. *The Unicorn from the Stars*, by Lady Gregory and W. B. Yeats.

1908.

Feb. 15th. {
The Man who Missed the Tide, by W. F. Casey.
The Piper, by Norreys Connell.
}

March 19th. {
The Pie-dish, by George Fitzmaurice.
The Golden Helmet, by W. B. Yeats.
}

April 20th. *The Workhouse Ward*, by Lady Gregory.

In addition to these plays, many of which are constantly revived, translations of foreign masterpieces are given occasionally.

It was not until the opening of the Abbey Theatre that Lady Gregory, Mr. J. M. Synge, and Mr. W. B. Yeats became entirely responsible for the selection of plays, though they had been mainly so from 1903.

Corrigenda.—P. 120, l. 5, for 'severe' read 'serious'; p. 143, l. 4, for 'prepared' read 'performed'; p. 176, l. 29, for '*their* own day' read '*our* own day.'

Lightning Source UK Ltd.
Milton Keynes UK
UKHW022042260722
406426UK00003B/57